Praise for *For Every Matter*
Preaching on Special Occasions

"Until now, preachers on certain occasions simply had to wing it. No guidance existed. Zink-Sawyer and Giver-Johnston have provided expert advice for these situations. One could buy a book on preaching for weddings or a book on preaching for funerals. This book will replace ten other books on the market, if one could even find an individual book on all of these topics. This volume contains the experience and reflection of two lifetimes of ministry and teaching. If students or young pastors buy this book, it will be ready to fall apart by the time they retire."

—Charles L. Aaron, Jr., director of the intern program,
Perkins School of Theology, Dallas, TX

"When I think of preaching on special occasions, I initially think of such occasions as baptisms, funerals, and weddings. This excellent book provides resources for these events and also for occasions that have distinctive characteristics even though they may not be the first to come to mind as special occasions: calls and commitments, congregational conflict, preaching among communities of older adults, holy days and holidays, crises, and situations beyond the church. With respect for exegetical and theological integrity, and with wisdom born from pastoral attentiveness, the authors help preachers move from specific contexts to the Bible. They describe the dynamics of special occasions in theological (and psychological) terms while positing possibilities for preaching. In addition to consulting the book as guide for particular occasions, I can imagine developing a sermon series based on the categories and chapters in this book. This volume should be a resource that preachers have on their desktops for easy reach. These occurrences knock at the

study door more frequently than one might imagine, and often enter the room with great force."
—Ronald J. Allen, professor of preaching, and of gospels and letters (Emeritus), Christian Theological Seminary, Indianapolis, IN

"This book will soon claim a place inches from the desktop of working preachers everywhere. Preachers—and those who teach them!—know how difficult it can be to preach fittingly for the varied life-situations, jarring or joyful, treated in this book's chapters. Inviting us to ask, *What is going on?*, *Who is listening?*, and *Where is God?*, Zink-Sawyer and Giver-Johnston trace theologically alert, sure-footed paths from situation to biblical text to pulpit, leading the way with pastoral wisdom and homiletical expertise."
—Sally A. Brown, Elizabeth M. Engle Professor of Preaching and Worship Emerita, Princeton Theological Seminary, Princeton, NJ

"*For Every Matter under Heaven* should be required reading for every student planning to enter pastoral ministry. I'm grateful to Giver-Johnston and Zink-Sawyer for offering up this straightforward, practical, and theologically grounded resource. Even pastors like me, who have been doing this work for many years, will find new ideas, resources, and guidance to which we can turn again and again. A copy of this book will always be kept in my office within easy reach!"
—Rev. Dr. Carol T. Cavin-Dillon, senior pastor, West End United Methodist Church, Nashville, TN

"*For Every Matter under Heaven* is a welcomed resource for seasoned pastors and new preachers. The broad consideration of special occasions from baptisms to holidays, a church's transitional moments to national tragedies provides a wealth of wisdom for nurturing and encouraging congregational life from the pulpit. Among the gems worth mining is the gift of multiple biblical texts appropriate to each kind of occasion which will help preachers make choices for their own context."

—Rev. Agnes W. Norfleet, senior pastor, Bryn Mawr
Presbyterian Church, Bryn Mawr, PA

"Beverly Zink-Sawyer and Donna Giver-Johnston give preachers clear and valuable guidance for preaching on special occasions and times of crisis, not normally found in the lectionary. Their framework for approaching these times, suggestions of scriptures and themes will assist the preacher to 'lean into' a message that will bring a word from the Lord. I would recommend this book as essential for new pastors and refreshing for those who have struggled with finding the right words to say."

—Rev. Dr. John E. Morgan, senior pastor, Williamsburg
Presbyterian Church, Williamsburg, VA

"*For Every Matter under Heaven* provides a much-needed resource for the times when preachers are faced with challenging pastoral circumstances. Zink-Sawyer and Giver-Johnston write out of a wealth of experience to support preachers in engaging a biblical text with the distinctive dynamics of particular occasions in view."

—Rev. Dr. Angela Dienhart Hancock, associate professor of
homiletics and worship, Pittsburgh Theological Seminary,
Pittsburgh, PA

FOR EVERY MATTER UNDER HEAVEN

FOR EVERY MATTER UNDER HEAVEN

Preaching on Special Occasions

BEVERLY ZINK-SAWYER
DONNA GIVER-JOHNSTON

Fortress Press
Minneapolis

FOR EVERY MATTER UNDER HEAVEN
Preaching on Special Occasions

Cover design: Kristin Miller (series design by Emily Harris)

Print ISBN: 978-1-5064-6579-1
eBook ISBN: 978-1-5064-6580-7

For our spouses, Steve and Brian, cherished
companions through all times and seasons.

And for our students and colleagues
who have answered the call to preach
on every matter under heaven.

CONTENTS

PREFACE

For everything there is a season, and a
time for every matter under heaven.
—ECCLESIASTES 3:1

The actual author of Ecclesiastes is unknown, but the superscription attributes the book to Qoheleth, commonly translated as
"Preacher." In the opening words of the third chapter of Ecclesiastes, the preacher reminds us that "for everything there is a
season." As we read on, we learn that the seasons include a time
to be born and a time to die, a time to weep and a time to laugh,
a time to love and a time to hate, a time for war and a time
for peace, and more. But no matter the season, the preacher of
Ecclesiastes reminds us, there is "a time for every matter under
heaven" (3:1). All our days are held in the hands of God. That
promise is echoed in the New Testament when the apostle Paul
proclaims the good news to the church in Rome that "neither
death, nor life . . . nor things present, nor things to come . . .
nor anything else in all creation, will be able to separate us from
the love of God in Christ Jesus our Lord" (Rom 8:38–39). As
preachers, we have the distinct privilege of speaking in the holy
and harrowing moments of human life and bearing witness to
the presence of God within them. This can be a tremendous
burden; it can also be an unparalleled joy. In either case, unique

challenges accompany our call to speak to those sacred seasons, especially when they occur beyond the usual pattern of Sunday morning worship.

As surely as the seasons unfold, that call to speak will come, whether we are ready or not. The telephone rings in the middle of the night, bringing news that one of your youth group members has been killed by a drunk driver while traveling home from college. The director of Christian education resigns abruptly the day before the youth mission trip, planned to begin with a commissioning in worship. The beloved pastor of a nearby church dies by suicide, and you are called to preach to a grieving congregation and neighboring church members. A church you once served invites you to preach for their centennial celebration. The local Rotary Club is hosting an interfaith Thanksgiving service in a diverse, suburban community and asks you to deliver the "message." A celebration is planned when the generosity of the congregation exceeds expectations for the campaign to transform the church's mission and outreach.

These are just a few of the real-life scenarios we have encountered in our years in ministry. All of them were marked by some kind of liturgical event, however brief the service or varied the venue, and each called for a word from the Lord in the form of a sermon or brief meditation. Unlike a typical Sunday worship led by a pastor who knows the congregation and usually has time to think and pray about the word of the Lord that is best conveyed in the service, many preaching occasions leave the preacher with little time for preparation and/or scant knowledge of those who will be in attendance. Some occur during weekly worship, and others are celebrated at different times and places, but all of these occasions call for preaching on a special theme or topic. The scenarios we've named are examples of some of those occasions.

Some are celebratory, such as weddings and baptisms, church dedications and anniversaries, commissioning services, and ordinations. Others are acknowledgments of a shared loss or time of uncertainty for the church or community, such as tragic deaths, natural disasters, or church closures. Other observances are less emotionally laden but nevertheless significant, such as national holidays or community celebrations. Still others provide opportunities for worship for those whose life circumstances preclude their participation in a local church.

Such occasions present the pastor with a difficult challenge: preach a sermon that is biblically grounded and also relevant to the particular occasion and to the listeners, often with limited preparation time given the demands of congregational life. Special occasions can easily render pastors overwhelmed and grasping for words to offer in the face of unique or unanticipated moments in their ministries. And yet it is often in such moments that people, some of whom are not regular churchgoers, are most open to and needful of a word from the Lord to make sense of life events or at least to find solace. These out-of-the-ordinary preaching occasions provide unique opportunities to deepen or renew the faith of those gathered and bring them into the presence of God.

Given the important yet challenging responsibility of proclaiming a meaningful word for special occasions, preachers are often in a quandary as to where and how to begin the preparation of a sermon. We offer this book to pastors and preachers (ordained and lay, seasoned and new) in an effort to provide brief but meaningful assistance in addressing the special occasions when we all will surely be called upon to preach. In addition to those who are already engaged in preaching ministries, we hope it will introduce seminary students to the kinds of special occasions they will encounter in their ministries and to a way of thinking about and addressing those occasions. In the conversations we have had over the years, we've both realized that little attention is given in homiletics courses to the preaching that occurs outside the pattern of traditional Sunday worship. And even when homiletics training does address preaching on special occasions (as we both have tried to do in our teaching experiences), time constraints on the theological curriculum prevent any sustained consideration of it. Our hope is to fill what is a gap in most homiletics curricula and provide preachers with a way of creating sermons that speak to the many occasions in ministry that occur within or beyond usual Sunday morning worship.

More than anything else, preachers need a reliable approach to thinking about the occasion and then finding an appropriate Scripture text that will serve as the basis for the sermon. An appropriate text might be found among the appointed lectionary texts for the day, or it might emerge from a thoughtful and prayerful process of reflection on the occasion. What is most important is that both the centrality of Scripture for proclamation and the work of God in the context of a special day are preserved. We intend for that "thoughtful and prayerful process" to be the major contribution of this book.

While a variety of other works address preaching on special days and occasions in various ways, this book is unique in offering a way of linking the circumstances of the occasion back to a text and from there forward to a sermon. Our goal is not primarily to tell preachers exactly *what* to say on a given occasion. The content of the sermon can only be decided in conversation with the context of the situation and the listeners, the text, and most importantly, God. Our goal, instead, is to help preachers discover a comfortable yet responsible approach that will enable them to *begin thinking about* what to preach and the texts that will convey that message, thereby strengthening the faith of individuals and worshipping communities. Special occasions and, particularly, moments of crisis can either render preachers silent or even unhelpful or offer preachers the opportunity to bring their listeners into the grace-full presence of God by preaching a relevant, even a healing or hopeful word.

That relevant word will emerge from consideration of the theological, pastoral, liturgical and other issues that define the occasion. The chapters that follow raise three questions that will help the preacher identify those issues and serve as the framework for thinking about special occasions:

- *What is going on?*
- *Who is listening?*
- *Where is God?*

With those three questions in mind, we have gathered a number of occasions under several evocative phrases taken from Ecclesiastes 3. The writer of Ecclesiastes captures well the range of emotions that accompany the many times and seasons of our individual lives and the lives of congregations. Some of those times move us to dance with joy, while others cause us to weep with sadness. Some times prompt tears of laughter; others move us to cry out in pain. Some seasons mark beginnings, while others represent endings. And some evoke several conflicting emotions as we acknowledge the reality of what has been and look forward with hope to what might be.

Before we begin, a few caveats that undergird our work must be named. First, one thing you will *not* find in this book about preaching is complete sermons. We occasionally reference sermons for illustrative purposes, but to include a complete sermon without knowledge of the larger context in which it was written and delivered would prove antithetical to our point. One of our main contentions is that every preaching situation and context is unique. That uniqueness renders—or *should* render—ready-made sermons of little help to the attentive preacher who seeks to be faithful to both the context and text for preaching.

Second, what we offer is far from an exhaustive treatment of preaching occasions. The occasions that might arise and call for an expression of worship that includes a proclamation of the word are as numerous as human experiences. Most preachers can look back on their ministries and name events they were called upon to address that they never could have imagined. We cannot anticipate, then, and even less prepare for, situations we might face in years to come. Thus, there is no way to address every preaching occasion that might arise. What we *can* do is help preachers be prepared for future challenges with a way of thinking about special occasions that will enable them to speak a word from the Lord whatever the circumstances. To that end, we offer reflections on a number of occasions as examples of how similar occasions might be addressed.

———

The idea for this book emerged from a course Beverly developed for seminary students and pastors. The idea was then nurtured by Beverly and Donna over years of a friendship that grew out of participation in our professional organization, the Academy of Homiletics. When the publication committee for the Working Preacher Books series—a partnership between Luther

Seminary, WorkingPreacher.org, and Fortress Press—expressed interest in the idea, we both knew that the "time," as the Ecclesiastes preacher would say, was right to pursue a book.

This book represents a true collaboration, as all of the decisions about the book as it unfolded were made together. In order to preserve our own voices and experiences, however, we each took responsibility for particular chapters: Beverly for chapters 1, 4, 6, 7, and 8, and Donna for chapters 2, 3, 5, 9, and 10. In the beginning of each chapter, we identify the writer so you will know who is speaking. We write as experienced pastors and professors, mindful of both the needs of congregations and the needs of those who serve them.

Donna is an ordained minister of word and sacrament of the Presbyterian Church (U.S.A.), having served small, medium, and large churches in rural New Jersey, small-town Ohio, and suburban Pittsburgh. She is grateful for a solid exegetical and homiletical education gained at Princeton Theological Seminary, where she earned an MDiv, and Vanderbilt University, where she earned a PhD in homiletics and liturgics, gained valuable experience instructing students in preaching courses, and wrote her dissertation about the call to preach. She continues to teach preaching courses for lay preachers as well as seminary students, with whom she shares her passion for and practices of preaching. But it was her nearly twenty years pastoring churches that challenged her and helped her learn how to preach on special occasions, from joyful weddings and baptisms to tearful funerals and crises, with pastoral imagination and love.

Like Donna, Beverly is an ordained minister of the Presbyterian Church (U.S.A.). She served churches in Pennsylvania and Tennessee for fifteen years before being called to serve as professor of preaching and worship at Union Presbyterian Seminary.

While her years in congregational ministry introduced her to the challenges of extraordinary preaching occasions, it was not until her years as a theological educator and visiting preacher that those challenges hit home. "Guest preachers" are more often called upon to preach for special occasions such as anniversaries, convocations, historical celebrations, and holy days in the lives of congregations. For many years she has felt an ever-growing need for this kind of book as she navigated challenging preaching occasions and contexts and is delighted to be able to join Donna in offering such a book to other preachers.

From previous writing experiences, we both know that it takes a village to "raise" a book! We are grateful to our "villages" for their support and encouragement during this project.

I, Donna, am thankful to God for this extraordinary call to the ministry of word and sacrament and to the congregations who have called me to serve as their pastor and preacher. I am grateful for my colleagues in ministry, who challenge, encourage, and pray for me, and for the students I teach and who teach me.

Like Donna, I, Beverly, am grateful for the privilege of serving God as a minister of word and sacrament for four decades and to the congregations I have served and the many congregations and community groups I have visited as a guest preacher. I am also grateful for the generation of students I have had the privilege of teaching and the colleagues in ministry who have shared their preaching ideas and experiences.

We both are grateful to the Working Preacher Books publication committee, especially to Karoline Lewis and her helpful review of the manuscript and to Beth Gaede for her excellent editorial work and, even more, her patient and pleasant guidance through this project. And speaking of patient, we cannot fail to thank our wonderful spouses, Brian Johnston and Steve

Sawyer, who have loved and supported us and traveled with us on this journey.

We cannot begin a book about unique preaching occasions without acknowledging the unique "season" in which we have been writing. The majority of this book has been written during the unprecedented time of the Covid-19 pandemic. This crisis, along with rising calls for racial justice, political polarization, and the endings and beginnings of wars, have made our petitions as people of faith for a word from the Lord more urgent than ever. Our hope and prayer for this book is that it will assist preachers in articulating the truth that no matter where we are or what we face, God's grace endures forever and bears us through every time and season.

Beverly Zink-Sawyer
Donna Giver-Johnston
Holy Week 2022

CHAPTER 1

From Context to Text

Beverly Zink-Sawyer

A time for every matter under heaven.
—ECCLESIASTES 3:1

For everything there is a season, and a time for every
matter under heaven:
a time to be born, and a time to die;
a time to plant, and a time to pluck up what is planted;
a time to kill, and a time to heal;
a time to break down, and a time to build up;
a time to weep, and a time to laugh;
a time to mourn, and a time to dance;
a time to throw away stones, and a time to gather
    stones together;
a time to embrace, and a time to refrain from
    embracing;
a time to seek, and a time to lose;
a time to keep, and a time to throw away;

a time to tear, and a time to sew;
a time to keep silence, and a time to speak;
a time to love, and a time to hate;
a time for war, and a time for peace.
What gain have the workers from their toil? I have
seen the business that God has given to everyone to be
busy with. He has made everything suitable for its time.

—ECCLESIASTES 3:1–11

In simple repeating phrases, these timeless verses capture the depth and breadth of the human life experience. Throughout the various rites of passage—"a time to be born, and a time to die . . . a time to mourn, and a time to dance . . . a time to embrace, and a time to refrain from embracing"—a reminder of the promises of faith remains: "[God] has made everything suitable for its time." As pastors and preachers, we are invited into those holy times in people's lives—from the beginning to the end and all along the way. In the face of such holiness, often we are moved to silence. And yet despite that often stunned silence, our call is to stand with people throughout all the times of life—in good times and in bad, in life and in death—and to speak a word, praying all the time, "Speak, Lord, for your people are listening." But the question is, as the apostle Paul so aptly expressed, "What then are we to say about these things?" (Rom 8:31).

The ancient Greeks distinguished between types of time using two separate words: *chronos* (χρόνος) and *kairos* (καιρός). *Chronos* refers to chronological or sequential time. We mark this quantitative *chronos* time with a clock and calendar. *Kairos* signifies a proper or opportune time that is qualitative. From our Christian perspective, it is the time that marks the activity and purpose of God. We reflect on *kairos* time in order

2

to understand divine presence and discern a faithful response. Every preaching occasion is set in *chronos* time and, therefore, shaped by the particular circumstances surrounding it: the reasons for the occasion, the people who gather to mark it, and the historic witness of our faith. But every preaching occasion also occurs in *kairos* time, God's time. When preachers try to discern what to preach on a given occasion, we begin with a thoughtful and prayerful reflection on the occasion and the issues surrounding it as well as the people who might be present. We then proceed to consider the theological issues at its heart as reflected in Scripture to see how God is at work in this *kairos* moment. Here is where preachers find their voices and the courage to speak a word of God for the people of God for every matter under heaven.

Every preacher faces special occasions within and beyond the pattern of Sunday morning worship. Of course, as Anglican priest Jeremy Davies reminds us, "no occasion could be more special than the regular preaching within the context of the holy common people of God gathered in a local church, especially when the assembly gathers for Word and Sacrament." But he goes on, "From time to time one steps out of the rhythm of the Sunday-by-Sunday engagement with the Word of God and [God's] people to concentrate on a particular issue, event, celebration or commemoration."[1] As homiletician David Schlafer adds, "Not every day is an ordinary day. There are a number of days on which homiletical 'business as usual' is not what is called for. We always gather to celebrate and seek the grace of God, but we do not always do so in the same way. Different concerns come to the fore at different times."[2] Some of those extraordinary days, such as Christmas and Easter, occur annually as part of the liturgical calendar. Others arise in response to local, national, or worldwide events or as part of congregational circumstances or celebrations. Still others, such as weddings and funerals, occur sporadically and, in the case of funerals, unexpectedly. Yet other preaching occasions come from invitations extended to preachers to participate in community worship services, held in various places for different reasons.

All preachers sincerely wish to offer their listeners in any context a meaningful word from the Lord. We want to be responsible in our interpretation of Scripture while connecting the promises found in it to a very real and perhaps unique contemporary situation, sometimes with little time to prepare. But few of us have been taught or have discovered a homiletical approach that enables us to accomplish those things. What do we do when we receive a call on Thursday to preach for a funeral service on Saturday while our Sunday sermon is still far from complete? Or when a local tragedy occurs on Saturday night, rendering our carefully crafted Sunday sermon moot? The call to preach often arises when we least expect it and have little time to construct a meaningful sermon in the midst of all the usual demands of ministry. And even when we have the luxury of time to plan and the pleasure of speaking for happy occasions, the challenge of finding an appropriate preaching text may remain.

The sermon-writing process taught in most mainline Protestant and Roman Catholic seminaries begins with an appointed biblical text, a reality that has been a blessing for preachers and congregations alike. But the downside of dependence on standardized Scripture readings as the starting point for sermons is that preachers may find it difficult to create sermons for occasions that have no specified texts. Where does the preacher begin when asked to offer a "meditation" as part of an ecumenical service celebrating the Fourth of July? How does one go about finding a text to speak a word of comfort from Scripture in the face of a community tragedy? What guidance is there for the preacher seeking to lead a congregation through the painful process of closing their church? The challenges for many preaching occasions that occur outside of ordinary Sunday morning worship often may include situations such as these:

- an unusual, sometimes fraught, occasion
- no appointed texts, or texts that do not seem appropriate for the occasion
- little time to prepare
- an unfamiliar group of listeners, some of whom might not be eager for a word from the Lord
- an unfamiliar place or a place not conducive to worship

What we propose in the chapters that follow is a way of thinking about the occasion at hand by raising the questions "What is going on?" "Who is listening?" and "Where is God?" By first answering these questions, the preacher will gain important insight for selecting an appropriate Scripture text. While moving from a situation to a text rather than the other way around may seem antithetical to what many of us were taught, we believe there is a way to make that move carefully, prayerfully, and responsibly to construct an essential bridge between context and text. For those who are lectionary preachers, we offer theological concepts, derived from consideration of the occasion and those who might be listening, that can serve as "lenses" through which to view the texts appointed for the day. Both the character of the day and the integrity of the stated readings are thus maintained. For those who are not bound or inclined to follow a lectionary, and for occasions that have no specified texts, we suggest Scripture passages that might speak God's word for that day.

What Is Going On?

It has been said that context is everything. That is especially true when it comes to the task of preaching. No sermon is ever delivered in a vacuum, separate from the multilayered, complex, often shifting context that shapes every word of the sermon and the larger worship event in which it resides. Preaching always occurs "within social, cultural, theological, and ideological settings," as homiletician Marvin A. McMickle states. He describes what he calls "environmental preaching," which is relevant to and informed by the setting in which it is being delivered and asks the question "How does the word of God speak to the congregation gathered at that time and place?"[3] Even what we think of as "regular" Sunday morning worship occurs against a backdrop of liturgical and natural seasons, current events swirling in the local community as well as the nation and the world, individual worshippers' personal issues and experiences, and any number of other issues that rest heavily upon the liturgical event. Those layers of issues are often magnified as we think about preaching occasions beyond Sunday morning. The reality is that no preacher, not even the most skillful one, can ignore the many contexts in which we live and move and exist; nor should we ignore them, for that would dishonor those gathered before us and deny our conviction that God cares about "every matter under heaven."

Preaching with a keen awareness of the human situation(s) in which it occurs is what homiletician David Buttrick calls "situational preaching" or "preaching in the praxis mode." It is a way of addressing congregations "where they are, relating experience to gospel rather than gospel to experience."[4] It is a kind of preaching "that addresses persons *in* lived experience and therefore, starts with a hermeneutic of lived experience. . . . True Christian preaching is not only a hermeneutic of texts, but a hermeneutic of human situations."[5] In order to identify the "human situations" that shape a given preaching occasion, the preacher can begin by asking several basic questions:

- What is going on here? What has given rise to this occasion?
- Why have people gathered? To mark an event or a special day? To honor, remember, or celebrate with an individual or group of people? To give thanks for an accomplishment?
- What is going on in the local community? In the nation and world?
- What is the mood of the occasion? Is this occasion one of celebration or shared grief?
- Are there historical or denominational issues that shape the occasion?
- Has this kind of occasion happened before? If so, what was the response on the part of individuals and the community of faith?
- What is the physical and liturgical—and even musical—setting?

Naming and answering a number of questions about the occasion enables the preacher to construct a "hermeneutic of human situations," as David Buttrick calls it, and serves as the first step in helping the preacher discern the appropriate tone for the sermon and find clues to theological themes leading to texts that might speak God's word to the listeners.

Who Is Listening?

Our approach to preaching on occasions outside of regular Sunday morning worship is deeply rooted in the experiences and needs of the listeners. Once preachers have taken a careful look at what is going on in a particular event in the life of the church or community, they must next take an equally careful look at the listeners who have gathered. As Methodist minister James C. Howell reminds us, "When we address people who bother sitting through a sermon, we need to grapple with their deepest dreams, wounds, and secrets."[6] That seems like an obvious piece of the homiletical puzzle, especially when addressing special occasions, but a deliberate consideration of the listeners has not always been part of the preaching curriculum. Seminary homiletics courses of the past taught students to craft sermons following meticulous exegetical work and by applying rhetorical principles, but the composition and complexity of the assembly, those who would hear that sermon, rarely were considered. There was an implicit assumption that the people sitting in church pews were monolithic and would hear and appropriate the sermon's message in the same way. That was never a valid assumption. First, there is no way of knowing exactly who will be seated in front of us for any preaching event and, second, there is no way of untangling the web of contextual and personal issues unique to each worshipper and what concerns weigh heavily on their minds and hearts. Even our own congregations, which may be fairly consistent from week to week and comprised primarily of people we know, offer surprises. Whether we preach to longtime members or guests, we cannot know all the challenges they are experiencing. Nor do we know how the listeners are responding to events in the world around us. Our responsibility as preachers is to *imagine* those listeners and what they might bring to the preaching occasion.

Over the past few decades, homiletical theorists have helped us think about and understand those who gather for worship. Much of the inspiration for this new approach to preaching emerged from liberation theologies rooted in Christian communities found in Latin America. Theologians and pastors in Latin American churches began their theological interpretations with the experiences and needs of the people among whom they ministered. That approach created a "bottom up" rather than "top down" perspective on the gospel and its teachings. In a similar way, homileticians who study African American and Asian American communities have increased our awareness of the essential role the listeners play in the effectiveness of sermons. Cleophus LaRue notes the ways in which unique "domains of experience" shape how African American communities hear sacred texts and stories. Understanding the multifaceted life situations of Black listeners is essential to the crafting of the sermon because they process the gospel "through life experiences rather than through codified theological formulations."[7] Eunjoo Mary Kim addresses a similar concern about Asian American communities, stating, "The listener-oriented perspective should be stretched to include an awareness of the ethnic diversity of the listeners and deepened to embrace culturally different communal methods."[8]

At the same time, new communicational theories arose, revealing the multifaceted ways in which individuals hear and learn. By applying it to preaching, as Leonora Tubbs Tisdale did in her book *Preaching as Local Theology and Folk Art*, the result has been sermons constructed so that listeners can better hear and appropriate the message. Tisdale encourages preachers to use the tools of ethnographic study to take a close look at the identities of those who compose their congregations to discern the symbols, norms, and values that shape communities of faith as well as individuals. That knowledge enables the preacher to construct what Tisdale calls a "'local theology'—that is, theology crafted for a very particular people in a particular time and place."[9] Information concerning the demographics (such as age, race, geographic location, and socioeconomic and educational status) and the ideological and theological perspectives of a congregation or gathering of worshippers can provide the preacher with clues for constructing that kind of local theology and, in turn, offer a sense of how a sermon might be heard.

In order to discern the needs of the listeners (and, eventually, the scriptural word that will speak to them), the preacher can raise several questions:

- What word do these listeners in this time and place most need to hear?
- How might the listeners be feeling? What do they bring to the service of worship? What might they be hoping for as they gather?
- What do we hope they will take away? How and in what ways might this sermon change the listeners and the worlds they inhabit?
- How do the identities of these particular listeners shape the ways in which they might hear the message?
- What hopes/dreams/fears do they bring with them to this occasion?

- What are they wondering about God? About themselves and their neighbors? About their communities and the world?
- What theological language and cultural symbols do they use and understand?

While no preacher can raise, let alone answer, all of the many questions that can provide insight into our listeners, taking the time to think about at least several questions such as these can lead us to a more relevant and effective message. We can even picture particular listeners or groups of listeners and imagine how they might hear the sermon we plan to preach. We can imagine a listener who is brimming with excitement over a job promotion . . . and one who has just been fired. We can picture a couple rejoicing over the news of their first pregnancy . . . and another who just lost a child. We can see a listener who has come back to the church after many years . . . and another who has given up on faith. The questions we raise and the people we bring to mind draw us closer to all the matters under heaven that our listeners carry to the preaching moment. As preachers entrusted with "the deepest dreams, wounds, and secrets" of those sitting before us, we have a holy obligation to seek a word from the Lord that speaks meaningfully to all who listen.

Where Is God?

While the issues related to the occasion on which we have been asked to preach and the concerns of the listeners who might be present are essential considerations, it is the theological themes arising from the occasion that will lead us to biblical texts. "The most important hermeneutical category" as we prepare to preach, homiletician Richard Lischer maintains, "is not socio-logical, psychological, or political—but theological."[10] It is the theological significance of the occasion at hand that makes it worthy of an act of worship and an opportunity to point to the work of God. As preachers, we are called to help the listeners make the connections between the events that mark our lives and the God who bears us through those events. We are called to "name grace," as theologian Mary Catherine Hilkert defines preaching: to name "grace found in the depths of human experi-ence."[11] An effective sermon should be a reminder of God's sav-ing work in Jesus Christ as revealed in the Scripture that bears witness to that work, enabling us to see where God is present and active in *our* lives and in the life of the world.

Preachers discern God's presence by engaging what Hilk-ert calls the "sacramental imagination" that "celebrates the mys-tery of God's presence here and now, summoning creation to a new future."[12] It enables us to move beyond our own theologi-cal assumptions—and those of our listeners—in order to point to the often surprising grace of God that upholds us through all the moments and days of our lives. It also reminds us that, as homiletician Karoline M. Lewis states, "in preaching, we are not providing information *about* God but creating an experience in which God will do what God does."[13] "A faithful preacher," Lewis goes on, "anticipates that the biblical text might reveal something about God never thought about before" and "won-ders each and every week what that something new might be."[14]

The "sacramental imagination" challenges us to seek the "something new" that God is doing and to build a theologi-cal bridge between the occasion (including those who might be present) and a text that conveys a meaningful word from God. It enables us to "name God in the world."[15] Such a theological bridge can be built by raising a series of essential questions or clusters of questions that will help us discern what the occasion reveals about such things as the nature of God and God's ways, our human nature in God's sight, what God calls us to be and do, and how we are to live as God's people. We can ask the following:

- Where do we see God being present and active in this situation? Where do we not see God and need to?
- How does this occasion reflect our theological commitments, especially our faith in the saving grace of Jesus Christ and the ever-present power of the Holy Spirit?
- What biblical and theological concepts might speak to those gathered for the occasion and give voice to the praise or lament, hope or celebration present within the listeners?
- What qualities of God, as revealed in the life of Christ and in the words of Scripture, are evident on this occasion?
- Can we point to the ways in which God has upheld us in the past in similar circumstances?
- How does the witness of the church reflect God's grace on this occasion?
- How might we all be changed and see more clearly God's presence and direction in our lives and community as a result of marking this occasion?

The questions we as preachers ask will be many and unique in regard to the occasion but will give rise to theological themes that suggest biblical texts that bear witness to God's grace in our lives and world.

Those biblical texts contain the ultimate assurance of God's involvement in every matter under heaven. It is in the events and teachings recorded in Scripture that we see the ways in which God has worked and will continue to work in the lives of God's people. "The Bible's great good news," says Episcopal priest Barbara Brown Taylor, "is that God is a palpable God, whose presence can be sniffed and glimpsed in every corner of creation."[16] We read the Bible, as Richard Lischer puts it, "not because it is filled with good stories but because it radiates good news about the character and disposition of God."[17] Proclaiming that good news about our God, who is with us and for us in each and every circumstance of life, is the ultimate goal of our preaching.

Having considered what is going on, who is listening, and where God is present and at work, the preacher will move on to seek a biblical text that speaks to the occasion and those gathered. The text, as James C. Howell suggests, "is a window into what God is doing in our lives and in the life of the world."[18] That text will also enable us to experience "revelatory moments," moments when we "notice, envision, overhear the presence of God, the hidden activity of the Spirit."[19] That is a tall order and great responsibility for the one who seeks a word from the Bible "on behalf of the church," as homiletician Thomas Long says. But, Long continues, "the preacher does not go with a blank tablet. The preacher comes from the community of faith, a community with its own theological traditions, social location, and prior understandings of the nature of both the Bible and the Christian gospel."[20] Given all that preachers carry with them to any text, the challenge is to step back and "serve as 'First Listener' to the text," as Old Testament scholar Ellen F. Davis describes the role of the preacher. "You are the first one to listen to how the text is speaking on this occasion, at this point in world history, in this particular assembly of the body of Christ."[21]

The process we propose for moving from context to text assumes, of course, that the preacher has a broad knowledge of Scripture and its vast array of stories and teachings. The preacher needs to be able to draw on that knowledge in order to retrieve an appropriate text or texts for the occasion at hand. This process also assumes that the preacher will do the hard work of careful exegetical study and apply the tools of critical scholarship lest texts be interpreted out of context or used as "proof texts" for one's prior assumptions. Only under the power of the Holy Spirit and after a time of "hovering" over Scripture can the preacher hear a fresh and appropriate word from the Lord.

Seeking and speaking the word of God for the people of God is always a "challenge and wonder," in the words of James Howell.[22] Preachers face that challenge and experience that wonder week in and week out, Sunday after Sunday, trusting that our words will bring our listeners nearer to the presence of God. Within and beyond the pattern of regular Sunday morning worship, however, there are occasions when both the awe and challenge are deepened by circumstances that shape the lives of individuals and congregations. On those days, preachers are called to name grace and give voice to the range of human emotions—love and hate, dancing and mourning, laughter and tears—that mark the seasons of life. They are days that remind us in special ways that God's care for us is evident in *every matter under heaven.*

CHAPTER 2

Baptisms

Donna Giver-Johnston

A time to be born.
—ECCLESIASTES 3:2

The writer of Ecclesiastes begins his ode to the seasons at the place where everything begins: birth. From that moment on, we experience the rises and falls, the joys and sorrows that mark human life. In the sacrament of baptism and other liturgical celebrations of new life, the church declares that, from the moment of birth, all our times are in God's hands. We are claimed as God's own, drenched with the cleansing grace that is ours through the saving work of Jesus Christ, and enveloped in the love of the community of faith. At the birth of the church on that first Pentecost, Peter invited everyone into the covenant of baptism to be sealed with the power and presence of the holy, life-giving Spirit: "For the promise is for you, for your children, and for all who are far away, everyone whom the Lord our God calls" (Acts 2:39). In such a time as this, on the occasion of new birth, preachers can name and claim the promises of our faith for all of God's children.

Given the joyful event of the birth of a baby, a preacher might think that writing a sermon for a baptism is as simple as A-B-C, as easy as 1-2-3. But the truth of the matter is that when you try to write the sermon, you realize that it is not as easy as it appears. Writing a sermon for a baptism (or any "out of the ordinary" occasion) is similar to putting together a jigsaw puzzle. We begin by identifying the contextual pieces, asking, "What is going on?" Then, we seek to find the pieces that reveal the situation of those gathering, asking, "Who is listening?" The third and final step is to put together the theological pieces that reflect the ways God's presence is promised in Scripture and in that particular time and place, asking, "Where is God?" These considerations will help you put together the sermonic puzzle to focus the process of delivering a sermon that is both faithful to a scriptural text and fitting to the particular occasion of a time to be born.

What Is Going On?

I remember a time early in my ministry when I received a phone call from a woman telling me the good news of giving birth to her first baby. Before I could offer words of congratulations, she asked, "When can we get our baby *done*?" I paused, not sure how to reply, and then asked what she meant. She said, "You know, dedicated in church." Now when those phone calls come, I just smile and say, "Let's get together and talk about baptism." Whether inquirers are brand-new to the church or have been away for a long time and are just now coming back, these meetings are good opportunities for teaching about baptism—as a celebration of life and as a sacrament of grace instituted by Jesus. In addition to teaching, the pastor needs to ask questions about the parent's understanding of baptism and why it is important for their child to be baptized and then to listen carefully to the responses. These conversations contain clues to the contextual issues that shape this baptism. From this conversation come further questions and reflections that will fill out the picture of your sermonic puzzle.

When preparing for a baptism, we first give attention to the one who is being baptized. Is he an adult who comes desiring to be forgiven for his sins and have his soul cleansed so he can live a new life? Is she a teenager coming to be baptized of her own accord, seeking something her lips tremble to name? Is he a toddler too heavy to hold and too rambunctious to wrangle and not too interested in baptism? Is she a baby who comes in the arms of her mother, who wants her child to be assured of eternal life? Is she a "Gerber" baby wearing a family heirloom gown or a precious baby with Down syndrome wearing a helmet? Of course, whoever they are, all come as children of God and in baptism will be blessed and marked as Christ's own.

In addition to the one being baptized, others are involved in the baptism, including the family. I always try to include any older siblings in the ritual. I will never forget when I baptized baby Jase, and his big sister, Harper, followed me all around the church as I introduced the newest member, making sure her baby brother was OK. On another occasion, I baptized baby Effy with water on her forehead, and her big sister, Lily, put her hands in the font and put the water on her own forehead. This grace of God was too good to waste; she had to have some for herself. Still another time, when meeting with the family of Ella (three years old) and Ava (six years old), I remember Ella was shy and hid behind her mom as I explained that I would put some water on her head. Being helpful, Ava said, "I can do it for you." I thanked Ava and said it would be very helpful if she could pour the water into the font, which she happily did. On the day of Ella's baptism, although Ella would not leave her daddy's protective arms, still I touched her head with water and claimed her as a child of God.

Once you have reflected on the people involved in the baptism, consider the physical setting. Will the baptism be outside in a river or in the sanctuary? Is there a baptismal pool or a font? Where does the font reside—in the center of the chancel or tucked away in a corner? Is there special significance to the font—the history and donor, the design and shape, the size and material of the bowl, clear or opaque? Consider the art, architecture, and furnishings of the church as they relate to baptism. One colleague of mine who serves a church in Cape Cod has created liturgical art featuring water that hangs in the sanctuary to remind people of their baptism. Another colleague shared that she preached at a church whose sanctuary was an octagonal shape. Historically, baptistries were octagonal, serving as a visual metaphor for the eighth day (following the seventh day of creation), which symbolizes the new beginning of a Christian life. Knowing the significance, she used the space to illustrate her sermon on the baptism of Jesus, preaching that here and now, surely the spirit of the Lord is upon us all, saying, "You are all beloved children of God, with whom God is well pleased."

Next, think about the historical context and denominational tradition. How are sacraments observed? What is the meaning of baptism, and how has it been ritualized in church history? In the history of your denomination? In the practice of your congregation? Is the baby sprinkled or immersed in water? Ponder the musical traditions. What hymns does the congregation sing regularly? Do they love to sing "There Is Power in the Blood" or "How Great Thou Art" or "Shall We Gather at the River"? The symbolic significance of a congregation's traditional practices contains important homiletical hints.

In addition, reflect on the liturgical setting. When in the worship service will the baptism occur? Will it be during the time in which we receive the grace of Christ or the time in which the congregation responds in faith? Consider how the baptism is enacted as a communal event. How is the congregation involved in the ritual? In our tradition, elders present the one to be baptized on behalf of the session. The congregation stands and confesses their faith with the Apostles' Creed and answers the question "Do you, as members of the church of Jesus Christ, promise to guide and nurture (names), by word and deed, with love and prayer, encouraging them to know and follow Christ and to be faithful members of his church?"[1] For the baptism of a child, I like to involve the children in the congregation as well, asking them, "Will you help (name) find his way to Sunday school?" and "Will you remind (name) that Jesus loves her?" The children don't just nod or say yes. Loudly and clearly, with no prompting from me, they spell out their answer: "Y-E-S!" The sermon is part of the liturgy and so needs to reflect the theological themes for the day. A sermon on the occasion of a baptism may proclaim in no uncertain terms that God's answer to the question of our belovedness is Y-E-S!

Finally, enlarge your scope beyond the congregation, and consider the local community, nation, and world. Think about water and what it represents. Are there issues around water? Maybe you live in an area of drought, where water is in short supply and high demand. Or perhaps you live in a place that has experienced floods, where water is dreaded and deadly. Be aware of places in our country and world where clean water is not available for everyone due to income inequality, racial prejudice, and other social factors. It is important to be mindful of the multiplicity of meanings that water might have for people. Preaching on the waters of baptism as a swiftly flowing stream might not be as well received by people whose homes were just flooded by a roaring river. In a community plagued by drought, people will be nourished by a sermon on the waters of baptism as the living water that Jesus promises will never run out.

The art of considering the one who is to be baptized and the other contextual issues is similar to finding and fitting together the corner pieces of a jigsaw puzzle, giving you an outline of this particular occasion on which people gather to hear a word proclaimed. But there are still more pieces of the sermonic puzzle to discover and fit together.

Who Is Listening?

Baptism is not just for the one being baptized. In fact, a baby will not remember this day. Baptism is also for those gathered for this occasion. And so it is important to consider the people who are watching and listening for a word from God to them. As part of one worship service in which I baptized a baby, I included a remembrance of baptism for the congregation. I invited people to come forward to the font, and I took some water in my hands and touched their foreheads, saying, "Remember your baptism and remember how much God loves you." I was deeply moved by the intimacy of touching the heads and looking into the eyes of people I knew and loved. I will always remember touching a man's bald head and then seeing tears fall from his eyes as I reminded him of God's love for him.

The pews are filled with all kinds of people: Parents who are eager to have their baby baptized to secure a place in heaven, just in case. Grandparents whose prayers have been answered at last, grateful to be blessed with the "cutest baby ever." Empty nesters who are nostalgic for their children now grown and out of the house. Others lamenting that they never had children or grieving the loss of a child. Some wondering if their daughter will ever find someone to have a family with. Others hoping that their gay son and his partner will find a welcoming church where the pastor would baptize their baby. Still others calculating how long this young couple will stay in the church after the baby is "done." Of course, babies are not the only ones who are baptized. I have baptized teenagers kneeling in front of the congregation on their confirmation. And I have baptized adults who desire to be baptized with their children or who are standing on their own before the throne of grace, finally believing that they don't have to prove their worth, just receive God's promises by faith.

No one comes to this occasion as a blank slate. Each and every person has a story to tell. And they wonder how their story relates to the story of God. They count on the preacher to tell them good news that matters to them and to show them where God is at work in their world today. In order to do this, we preachers need to know—or at least thoughtfully imagine—who they are, their stories, their successes and their struggles, their wonderings and their worries. While you may know some of the people, others you will not. Even those you know may have their own secrets, especially around issues of fertility and childbirth. What seems like a joyful baptism day for some could be a deeply painful experience for others. Allow yourself to wonder about what hopes and dreams, joys and tears they bring with them to this occasion. What message do these listeners in this shared time and place most need to hear? And how do the distinct identities of these particular listeners determine the ways in which they receive the message?

These people and more are sitting in your church pews when you stand at the font holding the child over the water and when you stand in the pulpit holding up the Scriptures. They are watching and waiting and listening for a word from God that speaks to them of the preciousness of this beloved one of God, the promise of renewal, the power of water, and the provision of grace that never runs out. As pastor, you can reassure them that there is mercy enough, grace enough, and love enough for you and for me and for all who believe.

Bearing in mind the situations of the listeners who gather to behold the gift of new life will help fill in other pieces of the sermonic jigsaw puzzle. Understanding the contextual questions of what is going on and who the listeners are, you can now attend to the theological question "Where is God in this particular occasion?" With the contextual corners and the contours of listeners in place, you can now search for the theological content and what needs to be communicated about the mystery of life and the promises of the Giver of life.

Where Is God?

Ryan was four years old and the fifth generation of his family in the congregation. He was no stranger to baptisms, having seen several of them. He was excited to be baptized and had practiced standing on the stool beside the font because he wanted to be a big boy! But on his baptism day, he decided to have none of it. He was fine through the words of presentation. But when it was time for him to come to the font, he dug in his heels and would not move. His mother's words went from gentle to stern but did not change his mind. His father literally dragged him forward as he screamed. He broke away from his father's grasp, scurried away, and crawled under the front pew, screaming, "No!" Despite their repeated attempts, his parents could not coax him out. As a seasoned pastor, Nancy let Ryan go for a while, and then she slowly walked toward him, bringing the bowl of water with her to the pew, and waited. Eventually Ryan stopped screaming and struggling, then slowly poked his head out from under the pew. Sensing he was ready, she knelt beside him, bowl in one hand, and put water on his head with the other. She baptized him right then and there, to Ryan's fascination, his parent's relief, and the congregation's delight. Realizing she had a captive audience, Nancy preached a word about baptism and what it meant: "If we knew what was happening in baptism, we would all run away. We just put a cross on this child's back."

Where is God in this ritual? Why do we baptize and what does it mean? Jesus himself was baptized, as all four of the Gospels attest. Mark tells the story this way: "In those days Jesus came from Nazareth of Galilee and was baptized by John in the Jordan. And just as he was coming up out of the water, he saw the heavens torn apart and the Spirit descending like a dove on him. And a voice came from heaven, 'You are my Son, the Beloved; with you I am well pleased'" (Mark 1:9–11). At the baptism of Jesus, God was in the dove descending on him and in the voice declaring his belovedness. In Jesus's baptism, the power of God is revealed for all to experience and behold. Knowing the power and the promise of baptism, Jesus implored his disciples to do so. At the end of the Gospel of Matthew, Jesus spoke these final words to those whom he called to carry on his ministry, "Go therefore and make disciples of all nations, baptizing them in the name of the Father and of the Son and of the Holy Spirit, and teaching them to obey everything that I have commanded you. And remember, I am with you always, to the end of the age" (Matt 28:19–20). These and other Scripture passages about baptism have been interpreted differently throughout church history and across denominations, thus resulting in an expansive theological spectrum. Baptism is the rite of initiation into the Christian community. Baptism is a cleansing from sin and a naming and claiming as God's beloved. Baptism is welcoming the newest member of the body of Christ and reaffirming baptismal promises for the congregation. Baptism is a renewal of God's covenant for all of God's people. Baptism is a dying to sin and rising with Christ to new life. Baptism is a sacrament in which water is a visible sign of an invisible reality of God's amazing grace and eternal love. Baptism is being sealed by the Holy Spirit and marked as Christ's own forever. In most Christian traditions, baptism is a ritual performed only once, but it can be reaffirmed repeatedly. Baptism puts a cross on our backs as we remember who we are—disciples of Christ—and it also puts a cross on our foreheads as we remember whose we are: beloved children of God.

The name for the Christian ritual is from the Greek word *baptizein*, meaning "to dip, to immerse, to plunge into the water." As in other religious rituals, Christian baptism reveals the archetypal meaning of water as that which drowns and destroys and at the same time cleanses and restores. Theologian Rowan Williams locates the meaning of baptism at the beginning of creation, when the spirit of God blew over the watery chaos and brought forth life that God saw was good. Williams attests, "Baptism means being 'in the depths': the depths of human need, including the depths of our own selves in their need—but also in the depths of God's love; in the depths where the Spirit is re-creating and refreshing human life as God meant it to be."[2] In baptism, as the water touches us, we in turn are in touch with the depths of the chaos of our own lives, even as we feel the breath of heaven that brings new life from God's love. As liturgical scholars Gerald Liu and Khalia Williams describe, "The Holy Spirit embraces us in delight and dedicated transformation [is] made possible by faithfulness to God and God's church."[3] In baptism, God goes first, speaking words of promise, often even before we can speak, and calls us children of the covenant. Here begins a lifetime journey of faith, when we gratefully live into the promises of the covenant.

This human rite of passage and the divine revelation of promises meet at the baptismal font. In *Mighty Stories, Dangerous Rituals: Weaving Together the Human and the Divine*, Herbert Anderson and Edward Foley make a bold and beautiful claim: "Bringing the child to baptism is an act filled with promise that the human mystery of a child and the divine mystery of grace will be united in a life of faithfulness that will not end in death." This is good news to celebrate. At the same time, Anderson and Foley point out, "bringing a child to be baptized is a sobering acknowledgment by parents that this child is simultaneously theirs and not theirs—their child and a child of God." In fact, "baptism is more than a hospitable ritual of welcoming; it is a divine act by which a child is claimed by God."[4] The promise of baptism is that the child becomes a child of God, and therefore, the child's story will be God's story and a part of the story of the community of faith as it seeks to embrace the Christian story and live into the promises of our faith.

A preacher is called to point to the promises of God in the scriptural witness. To help inspire your theological imagination, try wondering where you see God in this occasion. What does baptism reveal about the nature of God and about human nature in God's sight? What message does God speak in baptism? Where can you name grace?

The joy and challenge for a preacher on the occasion of baptism is to show that the water is more than a pool of water to splash the baby with, the child is more than a precious angel, the adult is more than a sinner in need of redeeming, the occasion is more than a ritual of human words and actions. The preacher who can reveal the depth of theological meanings of baptism will usher the one baptized and all the witnesses into the very presence of God. I remember during a worship service that included a baptism, during the children's sermon, I told them that I would put a sign on the baby's forehead to mark them as a child of God. After the baptism, a precocious young boy raised his hand and asked, "Where is the sign? I don't see anything on her forehead." This is the job of the preacher—to make the invisible sign visible, to make the unfathomable promise fathomable, to describe the indescribable grace of God.

Whether we like puzzles or not, the truth of the matter is, crafting an appropriate sermon for a certain occasion resembles putting together a puzzle—a difficult one. The good news is that if you have spent time attending to the *what* of the context, the *who* of the listeners, and the *where* of God's presence in baptism, then you can see the puzzle coming together and the picture beginning to emerge, but it is not complete as an opaque picture. Now it is time to consider which Scripture texts might speak an appropriate word to the listeners gathered on this occasion to hear a word of God for the people of God. As referenced in chapter 1, James Howell describes the scriptural text as "a window into what God is doing in our lives and the life of the world . . . a lens through which we truly see."[5] God's word becomes like a stained glass window or an icon, illuminating beyond itself to the Light of the World.

On this occasion, when we remember that God has designated "a time to be born," the preacher might refer to a concordance to find passages that speak of new birth and new life; for example, "So if anyone is in Christ, there is a new creation: everything old has passed away; see, everything has become new!" (2 Cor 5:17). The situation of the listeners may lead you to seek Scripture passages that remember the promises of God, such as, "For the promise is for you, for your children, and for all who are far away, everyone whom the Lord our God calls to him" (Acts 2:39). Or reflection on the theological themes of this occasion may call forth texts about baptism or water. Considering Jesus's own baptism and the voice from heaven declaring, "This is my Son, the Beloved," might lead one to preach that those baptized, like Christ, become beloved children of God (Matt 3:13–17; Mark 1:9–11; Luke 3:21–22; John 1:29–34). Then again, you may consider the prophets' words of promise to the people of Israel—"When you pass through the waters, I will be with you . . . for you are precious in my sight and honored and I love you" (Isa 43:2, 4)—and preach on God's relentless love for God's rebellious people.

In *Christian Worship*, liturgical scholar Gail Ramshaw lists several Scripture texts that are worthy of consideration for preaching a sermon in a worship service that includes the sacrament of baptism:[6]

Acts 8:14–17   The apostles who were baptized in the name of Jesus only received the power of the Holy Spirit when Peter and John laid hands on them.

Acts 8:35–39   After Philip taught him the good news of Jesus, in response, an Ethiopian eunuch asked to be baptized. After Philip baptized him, the eunuch went on his way rejoicing.

Acts 22:16   Ananias revealed that the early church understood baptism as a ritual that washes away one's sins.

Romans 6:3–5   Paul taught that in baptism, believers are buried with Christ in his death and raised with him in his resurrection.

Romans 6:22   Baptism makes believers slaves to God instead of sin.

1 Corinthians 10:1–4   Paul likens baptism to the covenant God had with Moses, whereby the waters of baptism are like the Red Sea, through which God led the people from slavery to freedom.

1 Corinthians 12:12   Baptism makes one a member of the body of Christ and serves as an entrance rite into the community.

Galatians 3:27–28   Baptism establishes radical equality in the community, where Jews and Greeks, slave and free, male and female are all one in Christ.

Galatians 3:29   Paul wrote that baptism establishes a covenant with God, like with Abraham, with responsibilities and benefits.

Ephesians 5:25–27 Baptism makes people holy and sacred, set apart for God.

Hebrews 6:1–5 Baptism is described as enlightenment, bringing people from darkness into the light, where they share in the Holy Spirit and taste the heavenly gift of the word of God.

1 Peter 3:20–21 Similar to the covenant God made with Noah after the flood, God makes a promise in baptism not to destroy but to preserve life through Christ.

Revelation 22:1, 14 Metaphorically, baptism is described as the river of life that flows from the throne of God, in which believers can wash their robes and, in so doing, be welcomed into the heavenly city.

Once you have selected a biblical text, the conversation begins between the preacher and God. Homiletician Tom Long corrects the image of a preacher sitting alone in the study, working with a biblical text, trying to wring out a suitable interpretation. Rather, the pastor goes to Scripture on behalf of a particular congregation, with their particular questions or concerns in mind. Long claims, "The preacher is a member of the community, set apart by them and sent to the Scripture to search, to study, and to listen obediently on their behalf."[7] Biblical scholar Ellen Davis offers some sage advice: "The role of the preacher is to step a little to one side and let the text have its say."[8] This process of biblical exegesis and waiting for a word will take time. But if you give it the time it needs, like a puzzle coming together, the picture that emerges will be worth waiting for. Homiletician Jana Childers, who aptly describes the process as "birthing the sermon," beautifully and powerfully claims, "Preaching is a mother who conceives and gives birth to faith."[9] May it be so for you as you celebrate new life and preach on the occasion of baptism.

Any one of these rich texts mentioned would allow you to name some of the questions in the minds of the listeners about the occasion as well as explore the theme of God's promise to surprise and bless and be with us always. When powerfully articulated in the words of the liturgy and sermon, as well as enacted in the sacramental ritual, the message clearly reminds and reaffirms the ultimate promise that there is a time to be born and that God has made everything suitable for its time.

Baptisms are meaningful any time of the year, but one of the most meaningful baptisms I remember was when I baptized the baby of a single mother who struggled with life and faith, especially with believing that she and her baby were loved by anyone, let alone God. She asked if I could baptize her baby on Easter Sunday. I hesitated, thinking about how full that Sunday would be with Scripture, special music, and the sacrament of communion. The choreography of the liturgy was complicated, and the church would be packed with people with high expectations for a glorious, even flawless celebration. As I considered all the reasons to say no, I realized that the day that we celebrate God's love defeating death, for all of us and for our salvation, was the perfect day to show what it meant to be a child of God, sealed by the Holy Spirit in baptism and marked as Christ's own forever. And so I said Y-E-S!

CHAPTER 3

Funerals

Donna Giver-Johnston

A time to die.

—ECCLESIASTES 3:2

The sobering reality that our days are numbered, as the Scriptures state ("a time to die"), stands in stark contrast to the hopefulness of birth expressed in the first clause of the couplet ("a time to be born"). Ecclesiastes is often read as a declaration of the "futility of life"—we are born, we toil, and then we die—or an invitation to enjoy the "pleasures of life": eat, drink, and be merry. But the significant wisdom from the preacher of Ecclesiastes is that "for everything there is a season" (3:1) and "[God] has made everything suitable for its time" (3:11). By the grace of God, birth and death are part of the continuum of life in God's presence. Our Christian faith calls us to live in the sure and certain hope of the resurrection to eternal life that is ours in Christ Jesus. Our funeral liturgies declare that our baptisms are complete as we pass from life to death to life eternal.

As preachers who seek to speak a word that honors one who has died and comforts those who mourn, we lift up that hope. And for those who have died, we claim the promise of eternal rest and that God's *lux aeterna*, light eternal, will shine on them and on those who loved them.

If you ask pastors whether they would rather do a wedding or a funeral, most (if not all) will say, "Give me a funeral any day." Why? Homiletician Tom Long's answer rings true: "At weddings, pastors sometimes feel trampled by overenthusiastic couples and their 'wedding handlers,' who can on occasion treat pastors as props, ecclesiastical bling in a schmaltzy fairy tale scripted by *Brides Magazine*." A funeral is much different. While most people come to the wedding ceremony secretly hoping it is short so they can get on to the reception to party, people come to the funeral service because they have looked into death's abyss, and they need to know how to go on living. Compared to the adiaphora of weddings, funerals are seen by pastors as an essential part of their calling. While a funeral may be preferred by pastors because of its significance and their vital role, that inclination does not make it easy. "The wildness of death, however, is not so easily managed," Long admits. "People stand back in voiceless awe over death's terror and mystery, and perhaps it is just their reticence that gives room for ministry."[1] It is into this space for ministry that pastors step, with humility, as they encounter holiness in the midst of death.

When Moses was overwhelmed with the mystery of the burning bush, he took off his sandals in respect for the holy ground he knew he stood on. It is on this holy ground of the mystery of death that we humbly take off our shoes and stand together with Moses, asking, "What shall I say?" In response, as God promised to be with Moses on his mission, so God promises to be with us. Although Moses had his brother Aaron to speak for him, on this holy ground of funerals, we preachers stand alone, without someone to speak for us. In the face of this *mysterium tremendum*, we realize the importance of the words we tremble to speak. And so, like Aaron, I will come alongside you for a while, walking you through the process demonstrated throughout this book. This chapter will first examine the contextual issues surrounding "a time to die," asking, "What is going on?"; then observe the situation of those gathered at a funeral, asking, "Who is listening?"; and finally explore the theological themes and scriptural texts, asking, "Where is God?" This process will equip you to preach a sermon that is faithful to the promises of our Christian faith and fitting to the particular occasion of a funeral, allowing you, like Moses, to speak truth to the powers of death, witnessing to the power of the resurrection that reassures us there is a time for every matter under heaven, even a time to die.

What Is Going On?

It has been said that nothing is certain except death and taxes. Death is one thing that all members of the human race have in common. And yet each death is unique, and we each respond differently to death. Some admit their fear of dying, as expressed lightheartedly by Woody Allen: "I am not afraid of death, I just don't want to be there when it happens."[2] Others affirm the resolute words of Mark Twain: "The fear of death follows from the fear of life. A man who lives fully is prepared to die at any time."[3] The truth is, most of us hold in tension a hearty fear and a humble faith as we consider the mystery of death. It is important for preachers to reflect on our own experiences of and feelings about death before we have to face the death of someone else and speak words of eternal life.

In *Mighty Stories, Dangerous Rituals: Weaving Together the Human and the Divine*, Herbert Anderson and Edward Foley poignantly remind us, "Whether we regard death as enemy or friend, as obliteration or transition, as a fact of being human or the consequence of sin, it is still an end." Death is a hard reality, and yet death is also a holy mystery, whose significance needs to be marked in religious ritual. Therefore, claim Anderson and Foley, "the grief and sorrow that attend it require rituals of storytelling and remembering."[4] A funeral is a time to remember the stories of the one who has died and the story of our faith that holds us in life and in death.

I remember the first time I saw a dead body. It was in seminary during my field education. My supervising pastor led me to the casket, said a few words about the man who had died, and then began talking with the family of the deceased. All I could do was stare at the coffin. I was so overwhelmed by the mystery of death that I was speechless. Since then, with over twenty-five years of ordained ministry, I have found my pastoral voice, but I still believe that on the occasion of death, there is "a time to keep silence, and a time to speak" (Eccl 3:7). So too, before preaching a word, pastors stand with the people on this holy ground, in silence, reflecting on the significance of this holy time.

I have been thinking a lot about death this year—not only because of the staggering number of deaths from the coronavirus pandemic throughout the world but also due to the higher-than-normal number of deaths in my congregation and my own father's death in November 2020. As I journey through grief, both personal and communal, I seek out and find comfort in books. Recently, I finished reading a touching book written by

Rabbi Steve Leder in response to the death of his father. In *The Beauty of What Remains: How Our Greatest Fear Becomes Our Greatest Gift*, Leder writes words that ring true from my experience as a pastor who regularly conducts funerals: "Often, when a person dies, it is up to me to tell the story of that person's life. The family is either too heartbroken, too conflicted, or just too exhausted to eulogize their loved one themselves. I consider this one of the greatest honors bestowed upon me. But that does not make it easy. How do I do it? How do I distill a person's essence, his or her story, down to a few pages and a few minutes?"[5] Knowing that as a pastor you have been or will be in that position as you approach the task of preaching for a funeral, you may be asking yourself that same question: "How do I do it?" And further, "How do I do it with compassion, competence, and love?"

The first task of a pastor who will be preaching at a funeral service is to consider the person who has died. A funeral for a person who will have people lining up to offer a word of eulogy is different from one for someone not many people will miss. I will never forget a funeral I did early in my ministry. I did not know the man who died or his family, who lived at a distance (and liked it that way) and came from out of town just in time for the funeral—with no interest in helping plan the service. With a sympathetic tone, I offered a glowing eulogy, praising this dearly departed man. After the funeral service, the son came up to me and said, "I don't know who you were talking about, but it wasn't my dad." I learned a lesson that day that has stayed with me ever since: make sure you know the person you are talking about, and tell the truth, even if it hurts. I have found that the phrase "none of us is perfect" is helpful to introduce a few things about the deceased that should be said in order for your message to ring true. Still, the person who has died, no matter who they are or what they have done in life, in death is named and claimed as a saint of God, made holy by Jesus Christ.

In *Ten Branches of Growth*, Kalen Bruce tells this illustrative parable, "Four Seasons of a Tree," from an unknown author:

> There was a man who had four sons. He wanted his sons to learn not to judge things too quickly. So he sent them each on a quest, in turn, to go and look at a pear tree that was a great distance away. The first son went in the winter, the second in the spring, the third in summer, and the youngest son in the fall.
>
> When they had all gone and come back, he called them together to describe what they had seen. The first son said that the tree was ugly, bent, and twisted. The second son said no–it was covered with green buds and full of promise. The third son disagreed; he said it was laden with blossoms that smelled so sweet and looked so beautiful, it was the most graceful thing he had ever seen. The last son disagreed with all of them; he said it was ripe and drooping with fruit, full of life and fulfillment.
>
> The man then explained to his sons that they were all right, because they had each seen but only one season in the tree's life. He told them that you cannot judge a tree, or a person, by only one season, and that the essence of who they are—and the pleasure, joy, and love that come from that life—can only be measured at the end, when all the seasons are complete.[6]

So too it is with a funeral sermon that reflects all of the seasons of a person's life, trusting in the promise of Ecclesiastes that for everything there is a season and that God has made everything suitable for its time.

In consideration of the person who has died, the preacher should meet with the family, friend, or significant other to listen to how they describe the different seasons of the life of the deceased. Rabbi Leder encourages family members to tell stories, which he describes as "making a story stew." Not only is this helpful for those writing a eulogy or sermon; it is also healing for the family, beginning the transformation process from tears of sorrow to tears of gratitude, from grief to glimpses of how the dearly departed live on in our memories. For others, this might be a transformation from anger to forgiveness of their not-so-beloved one. In *The Beauty of What Remains*, Leder writes about the last question he asks a family about the deceased: "If he could be there tomorrow with all of you, if he could stand up there and look out at you and say something, what do you think it would be?" Leder says that typically, after a time of silence, someone says, "I know exactly what he would say," and when it is shared, everyone nods in agreement. When Leder writes the funeral sermon, he ends with these final words shared by the family, claiming, "And those imagined last words are always an exquisitely beautiful, brief truth—the crystalline distillate of a person's story, a legacy of love."[7] Even if the deceased leaves behind a trail of tears, helping the family name their pain can be cathartic and necessary to begin the healing. Although funerals come unexpectedly into an already busy week of pastoral duties, it is advisable not to skip over this important step on your way to the sermon. Meeting with the grieving family or friends will help you know more about this departed soul, who is also a sinner in need of redeeming and ultimately, we trust, a sheep of the Good Shepherd's flock. As Christian preachers, we preach a theology not of good works but of God's grace, which has the power to save saints and sinners alike.

As each person who has died is unique, so too is each death. A funeral for a person who has enjoyed a long, full life is very different from one for a young child who has died. A death after a hard-fought battle with cancer is distinctly different from a death caused by suicide. An anticipated death of one in hospice care is different in many ways from a sudden death resulting from an accident. As you consider this particular death, reflect on its meaning in your congregation and, further, how it relates to death in the local community, nation, and world. Is this death the result of a local tragedy (gun violence)? Does this death reflect a disturbing national trend (drug overdose or suicide)? Is this death part of a worldwide catastrophe (coronavirus pandemic)? Is this death something that will hit the local congregation hard (cancer death of a beloved member), or will it come as a relief (the answer to prayers for an end to one's long suffering)? Be aware of the many different perspectives of and associations with death as you seek to understand what is going on in the context of a funeral.

After considering the person who has died, the preacher continues to attend to the contextual issues of death by bearing in mind the place where the funeral will be held. Will the funeral be held in a small funeral home or in a large auditorium? Will the funeral be a graveside service at a cemetery with the casket lowered into the earth? Will the service be on a boat on the waters into which the departed's ashes will be strewn? Will a memorial service be conducted after the internment? If so, will it be in the columbarium garden or in the sanctuary? If the service will be held in a funeral home or another place you are not familiar with, make sure you visit beforehand so you have a sense of the space. This will allow you to focus less on housekeeping and more on your pastoral care and proclamation of the word on the day of the funeral.

Funerals held in churches have special significance for some church members, for it is here in this place of sanctuary that generations have gathered to remember the promises of faith—babies have been baptized, youth have been confirmed, couples have been married, missions have been commissioned, sermons have been heard, hymns have been sung, bread and wine have been received in communion. A funeral that honors the sacredness of the space will nurture mourners for whom church is a place that provides significant strength for today and bright hope for tomorrow. I begin most church funerals by speaking these words of invocation: "Dearly beloved, we gather together at this time to mark the death and to celebrate the life of (name). We gather in this place of sanctuary to remember the promises of our faith."

Wherever the funeral will be held, consider the art, architecture, furnishings, and symbols in the space as they reflect the message of resurrection. Will the body be present in the casket, or will the ashes be in an urn? Will there be a candle lit? A pall placed? A flower laid? Will there be water in the font? Bread broken? Wine poured? Communion shared? A cross lifted high? All of these symbols will speak, so it is worth considering them carefully and even integrating them into your prayers and sermon.

By the time you are called upon to do a funeral, hopefully you are already familiar with how funerals have been ritualized in your denomination throughout church history and how they are typically conducted in your congregation. At this point, you can focus on components of the worship service, including the musical and liturgical settings. Consider what hymns the congregation typically sings at funerals. Do they sing "How Great Thou Art" or "For All the Saints," "Abide with Me" or "Swing Low, Sweet Chariot"? At locations outside of the church, where people may be uncomfortable with singing and unfamiliar with hymns, you might consider playing a piece of recorded music or having a soloist sing on behalf of the people. Be sure to ask if the family has a request for a special hymn. I will never forget the funeral of Sandy, a beloved woman and faithful church member who died after a long battle with cancer. She shared her strong faith, even until the end of her life, trusting in the promise of eternal life. When I met with her in the hospital to plan her funeral, she asked that it be a joyful celebration of her life, with the choir singing "I'll Fly Away" and playing tambourines. For some people, this would have seemed odd, but for Sandy, it was a fitting celebration of her faithful life. Along with the music, the prayers are a significant part of the service, as they offer pastoral assurance: "O God, your love cares for us in life and watches over us in death. . . . May we remember Sandy in love, trusting her to your keeping until the eternal morning breaks."[8]

As you craft the liturgy, ensure that there is a time to mark the death and to celebrate the life of the deceased. Is there space in the liturgy for lament and silence as well as thanksgiving and praise? Is there room in the service for family and friends to read Scripture or offer eulogies to the deceased in remembrance of their life? As you consider the wishes of the family and reflect on them pastorally, you will be better able to answer the question "What is going on?" All of these matters will be factors in the preparation of your sermon.

The sermon is not limited to a eulogy of the deceased, because the gospel story does not end in death. Scripture tells the story of resurrection and victory over death. And this story needs to be told without hesitation throughout the worship service—in music, prayers, and sermon. The sermon has the power to bring healing and hope by connecting the story of the deceased to the biblical story of our collective faith, connecting the story of death and grief to the story of God's relentless love and resurrection hope.

Who Is Listening?

After reflecting on the person who has died, the place of the funeral, and the liturgy of the service, the next task of the preacher is to consider the listeners. Try to envision who will be gathering for the funeral. The people who come to a funeral have in common a relationship with the deceased, but they differ in how and why they come. Some people in the pews knew the person well and are grieving their death, needing to hear words of comfort. Some people come out of duty or respect for the dead, whether or not they shared a close relationship, or to support the people who were close to the person who died, needing to know what to say to the mourners. Others come because they feel guilty about something they said or did to cause hurt that was not resolved, and they need to be forgiven. Some may be coming with doubt or cynicism; some may be agnostics or atheists. Some may be coming with existential questions, trying to make sense of the mystery of death. Still others come to give thanks for their loved one's relationship with God and to hear the sure and certain promises of eternal life.

Family members of the deceased will typically sit in the front pew, close to the casket or urn, with tears in their eyes and grief etched into their faces. Some may be glad the suffering of their loved one is done; others are wishing for a little more time. Some may be numb, not sure how they are feeling. All are a little shaken as they come face-to-face with death, hoping to hear a word that will bring them the peace that passes understanding, the peace the world cannot give.

I consider it an honor to stand with people on such holy ground and preach, in no uncertain terms, the promise of the gospel. But truth be told, each funeral is also an emotional event, as I profoundly grieve the loss of people with whom I have had a personal relationship, often a close one. Preaching at these funerals is both a heavy burden and a holy blessing. Such was the case with the unexpected death of Ross, a well-respected elder, finance committee chair, and wise and trusted confidant of mine. Throughout his life, Ross was a committed and gifted choir member. He had a deep bass voice that gave depth and resonance to choral anthems. At nearly every Good Friday Tenebrae service we held over the years, Ross sang a powerful solo that left us all with chills, some even with tears. He sang, "They crucified my Lord, and he never said a mumblin' word. Not a word. Not a word. Not a word." As Ross's family and I sat together in the hospital following what they think was a massive stroke from which he never regained consciousness, we watched him lie in silence, hoping against all evidence to the contrary that he would say something, anything, to end this nightmare. But he never said a word—not a word. "Death obviously brings silence to those who die, but it also stills the voices of those around the dead," rightly notes Tom Long, "and the pastor is there with needed wisdom, ancient words of comfort and hope, personal words of remembrance and love."[9] It is on this holy ground that we stand with those who are grieving and speak the words they need to hear—words of healing and hope, promise and peace, resurrection and eternal life—words that Ross knew by heart and sing on beyond the grave.

In searching for the words the silent listeners need to hear, the pastor needs to imagine what the mourners would say if they could speak. Imagine how the listeners are thinking and feeling. What are they wondering about—about the deceased, about death, about God? What do they bring with them to the occasion (maybe anger, sadness, grief, shame), and what do they need to take from it (grace, mercy, comfort, assurance, faith)? Ask yourself what word the listeners most need to hear, keeping in mind that funerals are not for the dead, but for the living.

The church can provide a worship service that proclaims in no uncertain terms the truth that death does not have the last word. God does—and it is a word of life, eternal life. The preacher's call is to preach the gospel, trusting that in the face of death, this offers the deepest comfort of all. Church members come to be a part of the congregation, to be reminded of the promises of faith—in Scripture, sermon, and song—and to be a witness to the community of believers. In one church I served, we started what we called a "resurrection choir"—church members who came to funerals to sit in the pews and to sing the hymns that the grieving family might not be able to sing for themselves: "For all the saints, from whom their labors rest . . . we feebly struggle, they in glory shine. Alleluia, alleluia!" Anderson and Foley remind us of the value of the congregation: "The presence of a faith community absorbs grief and transforms it into hope within a framework of ongoing trust in the promises of God."[10] The faith community witnesses to this truth, reminding us of the promises of faith, lifting its voice when we ourselves cannot sing, joining with the celestial choir: "'Tis grace has brought me safe thus far, and grace will lead me home."

Where Is God?

After you have gotten to know the deceased person through the family's remembrances and your own personal reflections and considered the situation of the people listening, then comes the time for theological reflections about death and God's promises of life. This reflection embraces the good news of the gospel and the story of faith as passed down from generation to generation. Anderson and Foley offer some humorous but helpful wisdom:

> You can mess up at a wedding, a pastoral friend of ours has observed. People will laugh about how silly the pastoral minister was at the wedding, but it will probably not significantly affect the success or lack of success in the marriage. But . . . you should do everything in your power not to mess up at a funeral. The words we say and how we say them, the scripture passages we read, the way the building looks, our presence and bearing, which brings comfort and acceptance in the midst of chaos, and the hospitality we provide the family and friends—all these things help people at tragic moments of loss when they must reconstruct their reality without someone they love.[11]

Chances are good that pastors will not "mess up at a funeral" if they help listeners "reconstruct their reality without someone they love." We do this by proclaiming a life-giving sermon that considers the needs of the listeners and speaks to the particular context. But we cannot do that without theological reflection. Discerning the theological themes that define a preaching occasion is essential in building a bridge between the occasion itself and the biblical text or texts from which the preacher will develop a sermon. Without this essential theological piece of the process, the preacher will be unable to find appropriate texts and craft suitable sermons that speak to the occasion and the needs of the listeners.

Laurence Hull Stookey identifies the truth that "to be deeply Christian is to know and to live out the conviction that the whole human family dwells continuously at the intersection of time and eternity. . . . God is perpetually at work in all of creation."[12] Further, as Christians who affirm the truth of the incarnation and who with the psalmist praise the God who "knit me together in my mother's womb" (Ps 139:13), we believe that human history and divine holiness are intricately intertwined. Still, we acknowledge that some experiences, especially death, can obscure God. Then it is the call of the preacher to stand at the intersection of time and eternity, helping to reveal the holy hiddenness of God by attending to the occasion and reflecting on the theological themes that can help point us to God's promise even here, even now. The theological themes of a funeral are revealed by asking questions such as these:

- Why did they have to die? Is the deceased in heaven or hell? Is his spirit still with us?
- What is heaven like? Is she with previously deceased loved ones? Are they at peace?
- What is death? Why is life finite and fragile? How does this death reveal my mortality?
- How can we not give in to despair? Where is our hope? What can we say for sure?

No preacher can answer all of the questions that people bring with them to a funeral service. Nor can we wipe every tear or take away every pain that weighs down the mourners. But we can take seriously their experience and validate their feelings of loss by honestly reflecting on these questions that weigh heavy on the hearts of our listeners. And perhaps most importantly, we can locate their story within the story of holy Scripture, witnessing to the truth that in life and in death, we belong to God. The theological promise of God's presence in life and in death helps mourners hold on to hope for an ultimate reunion with the deceased, even as they give thanks for the memories that will abide with them long after their loved one is gone. Now that we know the stories of the deceased and the listeners and the questions the mourners may be asking, it is time to go to God's story, weaving together the earthly and heavenly stories to create a sermon.

With these theological questions in mind, the preacher will go to Scripture, searching for words of comfort and strength. Consider Jesus's message to his disciples as he was leaving them: "Peace I leave with you; my peace I give to you. Do not let your hearts be troubled, and do not let them be afraid" (John 14:27). Or Isaiah's promise: "Have you not known? Have you not heard? . . . Those who wait for the Lord shall renew their strength, they shall mount up with wings like eagles" (Isa 40:28, 31). Or Paul's assurance: "If we live, we live to the Lord, and if we die, we die to the Lord; so then, whether we live or whether we die, we are the Lord's" (Rom 14:8). Variations on these themes of peace and trust can be woven through the liturgy and sermon, reminding the mourners that yes, there is a time to die, and yes, the God of peace and strength has made everything suitable for its time.

Pastors would do well to ask family members if they have a favorite biblical passage or know of one that their deceased loved one trusted in and leaned on. I remember a widow sharing with me her husband's Bible from which he read every morning. She was surprised to find that he had clearly marked verses that were near and dear to his heart. Reading verses that were meaningful to the deceased is a powerful witness to their faith for those gathered to mourn their death. Such texts can be preached as a message from the deceased to the family left behind, offering reassurance of their deep and abiding faith that endures beyond the grave.

While it is always a good idea to ask the family members if they or their deceased loved one had a favorite biblical passage, often family members will ask you, the preacher, to choose an appropriate one. Here are some trusted and true pericopes for a funeral:

Psalm 23:1   "The Lord is my shepherd, I shall not want."

Psalm 90:12   "So teach us to count our days that we may gain a wise heart."

Psalm 103:2   "Bless the Lord, O my soul, and do not forget all God's benefits."

Psalm 121:1-2   "I lift up my eyes to the hills—from where will my help come? My help comes from the Lord, who made heaven and earth."

Psalm 130:1-2   "Out of the depths I cry to you, O Lord. Lord, hear my voice!"

Psalm 136:1   "O give thanks to the Lord, for God is good, for God's steadfast love endures forever."

Psalm 139:1-12   "Where shall I go from your spirit? . . . If I ascend to heaven, you are there."

Isaiah 40:1-11   "Comfort, O comfort my people, says your God."

Isaiah 40:28–31	"Those who wait for the Lord shall renew their strength."
Isaiah 65:17–25	"For I am about to create new heavens and a new earth."
Luke 23:39–43	To the criminal on the cross pleading for mercy, Jesus said, "Truly I tell you, today you will be with me in Paradise."
John 11:17–27	To Martha, grieving the death of her brother Lazarus, Jesus said, "I am the resurrection and the life. Those who believe in me, even though they die, will live."
John 14:1–6, 25–27	To his disciples he would be leaving, Jesus said, "Peace I leave with you; my peace I give to you. . . . Do not let your hearts be troubled, and do not let them be afraid."
Romans 8:31–39	"Neither death, nor life . . . nor anything else in all creation, will be able to separate us from the love of God in Christ Jesus our Lord."
Romans 14:7–12	"If we live, we live to the Lord, and if we die, we die to the Lord; so then, whether we live or whether we die, we are the Lord's."
1 Corinthians 15:53–58	"Death has been swallowed up in victory. . . . Thanks be to God, who gives us the victory through our Lord Jesus Christ."
Revelation 21:1–4, 22–25	"Then I saw a new heaven and a new earth . . . death will be no more; mourning and crying and pain will be no more."

These Scripture readings help us answer the question "Where is God?" at the time of death. Long reminds us that funeral preachers "go to Scripture to hear the word of life and hope, but they do not go as blank tablets. They take with them the circumstances of the funeral—*this* death, *these* people, *this* loss, *these* needs." With these particular people in mind, the preacher goes to Scripture and listens for what God may be saying. As you know, sometimes we hear clearly, and other times we have to sit in silence, struggling to hear that still, small voice. Just like Moses went to the mountaintop with the questions and concerns and complaints of the Israelites, so the preacher goes to God's word with the context, listeners, and theological questions in mind and listens on their behalf. Just like Isaac wrestled with the angel of God all night until he received a blessing, so the preacher may have to wrestle with the biblical text until what emerges is the good news of the presence of God here and now and forevermore. This process of listening to the biblical text on behalf of your listeners and waiting for a word from God will take time. But with faithful listening, what will emerge will be worth waiting for. In the end, Long concludes, "the sermon happens when the preacher, who has gone to the Bible from the people and on behalf of the people, now turns and goes back to the people and is a faithful witness, telling them courageously and truthfully what has been heard."[13] In the case of a funeral, what needs to be proclaimed to people sitting in sorrow and facing the mystery of death is a word of steadfast hope of the resurrection to eternal life.

In Exodus 3, Moses, standing on the holy ground before the burning bush with his sandals off, inquired of God what he should say. By what name, he should say to the Israelites, is this God called who sent him? God said to Moses, "I AM WHO I AM. . . . Thus you shall say to the Israelites, 'I AM has sent me to you'" (Exod 3:14). Inspired by this story, we preachers can confidently stand on the holy ground of a funeral and announce, "The God who is called I AM—not I was or I will be—is the same God who is with us here and now, whose love cares for us in life and watches over us in death."

Henri Nouwen wrote *A Letter of Consolation* to his father after his mother's death, believing that consolation is to be found "in the firm conviction that reality can be faced and entered with an open mind and an open heart, and in the sincere belief that consolation and comfort are to be found where our wounds hurt most."[14] Nouwen reminds us that if a funeral is to bring consolation to those who mourn, then the preacher should not hesitate to name the pain of "where our wounds hurt most" but should courageously face the reality of loss by using the language of lament to bring healing. Skipping over the pain of death to pronounce the good news of resurrection will be heard as "cheap grace" and will not comfort listeners or sustain their faith. Like Jesus—who, upon hearing of the death of his friend Lazarus, wept before proclaiming the resurrection—we preachers need not be afraid to name and even feel the pain, even as we preach the promise of a time when "God will wipe every tear from our eyes; death will be no more; mourning and crying and pain will be no more" (Rev 21:4).

Funeral sermons are not one-size-fits-all. They need to weave together the human story of the deceased and the sighs of despair of the community with the Christian story of hope and eternal promise. Christian funeral sermons speak the truth of God's eternal love. Even as we mourn the death of a person we love, we rejoice that their baptism is complete in death and give thanks for the gift of a life now returned to God, from whom all blessings flow.

CHAPTER 4

Calls, Commissionings, and Commitments

Beverly Zink-Sawyer

A time to plant, and a time to
pluck up what is planted.
—Ecclesiastes 3:2

The mission of the church, at its core, is to spread the gospel, the good news of Jesus Christ. Agricultural images are often used in the New Testament to describe that mission. Jesus commanded his disciples to "go and bear fruit" (John 15:16). He spoke of the kingdom of heaven as a seed growing in secret. In the first letter to the Corinthians, Paul describes the young church as having been "planted" by him and "watered" by Apollos but "grown" by God. For two thousand years, members of the church have continued to "plant" by means of teaching, preaching, and ministries of care. They also continue to "pluck up" or harvest what was planted, as individuals who have been shaped by the work of planting accept roles and responsibilities as leaders of the church. All of that planting and harvesting is made possible by means of the time, talents, and tangible resources offered by individuals and congregations to the glory of God. And so the divinely ordained cycle of planting and harvesting through the work of the church goes on.

Celebrations of the gifts and graces that are given to individuals to be used in the service of God and the church are important moments in the life of any community of faith. As reformer Martin Luther reminded us, we *all* are called to Christian vocation by virtue of our baptisms. But all the baptized are called at times to serve the church in special ways. Congregations seek God's blessing—and confer their own—upon people and things set apart for such service by means of liturgical celebrations.[1] Seminary graduates are ordained to a variety of ministries of the church. Members of congregations are commissioned to serve as teachers and missionaries. Lay leaders are installed, or even ordained, to serve in various offices to carry out the work of congregations and governing bodies. Young people are invited to confirm for themselves the promises their parents made for them as children, and new members are welcomed into congregations. Tangible gifts of money, buildings, and furnishings are dedicated for sacred use. The work and witness of congregations are celebrated by means of anniversaries and homecomings. New congregations are planted to begin another cycle of ecclesiastical life.

The celebration of such special events may become the focus of a Sunday morning worship service or a service held at another time. Those gathered for the celebration will include church members and perhaps others who represent the wider church and community. The terminology used to describe those entrusted with the work of the church and the form of the celebrations will vary among Christian traditions, but all congregations and denominations gather from time to time for special occasions to celebrate *calls* (to ordained ministry), *commissionings* (for special service to the church), and *commitments* (of our lives and resources). They are different expressions of the same impulse: our desire to serve God through the mission of the church. However they occur and whatever they sanctify, such occasions celebrate the church's work of planting and harvesting in response to Christ's command to "go and bear fruit."

Calls

Something poignant and moving occurs when a community of believers petitions the Holy Spirit to empower those who have answered the call to serve God and God's people in a special way. Those of us who have knelt or stood before a congregation and felt the weight of their hands placed upon our heads and their prayers placed upon our hearts can testify to the spiritual power conveyed in the act of ordination. From the beginning of the priestly tradition in the Old Testament, leaders of the community of faith have been chosen by God and have had their leadership acknowledged by the community. In the New Testament, Jesus called disciples to learn from him and carry out his mission. The early church continued those traditions by setting apart the leaders who they believed had been called by God, a practice that we embrace today as we acknowledge those among our own who have been called to plant and harvest as workers in God's fields of ministry.

What Is Going On?

Most denominations ordain those who have answered the call of God to function as the church's leaders.[2] Some individuals will be ordained as pastors, priests, or ministers to serve the church "for the sake of good order," as Methodist bishop William Willimon states, and "to witness, to teach, to heal, and to proclaim to the church on Sunday so that all the baptized may witness, teach, heal, and proclaim during the rest of the week."[3] Others will be ordained to lay offices such as elder or deacon. What is going on when the church gathers for a service of ordination is the acknowledgment that God calls and empowers individuals who have been formed by the community of faith, who will now go out to lead communities in forming others. The occasion, then, must be focused primarily on God's action and only secondarily on our human response.

Sermons for ordinations are similar to those for occasions such as weddings and funerals. The reason for the gathering is to recognize an individual or individuals at a significant life transition: marriage, death, or the beginning of ministry. But those transitions occur within the larger context of the gathered community and the church's witness. Thus, the sermon must move "through and beyond" the individuals, as Episcopal priest and homiletician David Schlafer asserts. Those being ordained are "not so much the *focal point* of the service as they are its *point of departure*" on the way to a celebration of community vocation.[4] As with every worship service, this one too is about *God* and not about *us* (or one of us)—about what God has done and continues to do within the community of faith. "What everyone is there to celebrate," Schlafer goes on to say, "is not *my* ministry, *our* ministry, *their* ministry—but the ministry of *Christ* to his Body, and through his Body to the world."[5]

Who Is Listening?

Those who are listening at a service of ordination will probably be a wide-ranging group of individuals who are seeking to be part of Christ's body in the world. The individual(s) being ordained may well bring a range of emotions: gratitude for God's call and the gifts to pursue it, relief after years of arduous study and ecclesiastical trials, excitement for the ministry about to unfold, and some trepidation about stepping out into whatever lies ahead. Those who have come to celebrate the ordination will probably include members of the congregation where the ordination takes place as well as representatives of the wider faith community. Present will be the pastors, church school teachers, and youth leaders who planted and nurtured the one being ordained; family members and friends; new colleagues in ministry; and denominational representatives. Most of the listeners will welcome the candidate's choice of vocation, but some will accept it with a degree of skepticism or concern. Most of the listeners will be conversant with the language of faith, but some will be unfamiliar with what appear to be mysterious words and actions. Most will come with great pride and gratitude for the one whom God has chosen from their midst, but a few might regret that because of their life circumstances or ecclesiastical barriers due to gender or sexual orientation, they were not able to answer a similar call. No matter the emotions carried by individual listeners, the day will be marked by feelings of joy and thanksgiving and hope for the future.

Where Is God?

We discern the work of God most obviously in the type of call that has claimed the individual who stood up, as Isaiah did, and said, "Here am I; send me!" (Isa 6:8). But as I learned from many years of working with seminary students, calls come in different shapes and sizes. Some are planted early in life and are like the seed in one of Jesus's parables, growing quietly without the farmer's understanding of how, then suddenly and unexpectedly coming to fruition. Others bloom early and are nurtured for years. Still others spring forth from what appeared to be fallow ground, surprising even the one who has been called.

The Bible recounts a similar variety of "call" stories in both the Old and New Testaments, one of which might reflect the experience of the one being ordained. We can point to

- Abraham, who answered God's call late in life (Gen 12:1–9);
- Moses, who was startled by the voice of God from a burning bush while minding his own business and his flock of sheep (Exod 3:1–12);
- Samuel, who was called and nurtured from childhood (1 Sam 3);
- Esther, who spoke out bravely to save her people (Esth 8:1–17);
- Isaiah, who received a vision of God in the temple (Isa 6);
- Mary, who was chosen to bear the Christ child (Luke 1:26–38);
- Jesus, who was anointed at his baptism to fulfill God's work of redemption (Matt 3:13–17; Mark 1:9–11; Luke 3:21–22);
- the first disciples, who closed tax books and dropped fishing nets to follow Jesus (Matt 3:18–22; Mark 1:16–20; Luke 5:1–11, 27–28);

- the women who were shocked to find the empty tomb and would then "go and tell" the others the good news of the resurrection (Matt 28:1–10; Luke 24:1–9);
- Paul, who was transformed from persecutor of Christians to preacher of the gospel on the road to Damascus (Acts 9:1–31).

Beginning a sermon for an ordination with a biblical story of a call similar to that of the one being ordained acknowledges the surprising ways God works in our lives and in the life of one particular individual. But from there, the preacher needs to move "through and beyond" the individual's story to the places where God *is* and *will be* at work through the community of faith under the leadership of this newly ordained servant. By the power of the Holy Spirit, God was, is, and promises to be with the one whose particular chosen vocation is pastoral ministry, but that vocation emerged from and will be expressed in the context of the community of faith. William Willimon defines Christian ministry as first "an act of God" and second "an act of the church."[6] The service of ordination in the Presbyterian Church opens by declaring that in baptism, the candidate was "claimed by the love of God, clothed in the grace of Jesus Christ, and anointed with the gifts of the Holy Spirit" but also "called by God through the voice of the church."[7] Other traditions may use somewhat different language, but all agree on the essential participants in the process of call: God, the individual, and the community of faith, all inspired by the work of the Holy Spirit. Thus, any appropriate message on the occasion of ordination must resist the temptation to devolve into a sentimental celebration of the ordinand, as David Schlafer reminds us, and must instead maintain the concept of shared Christian vocation as "the primary facet of grace" that is at work in the occasion. Ordinations are not "award ceremonies," Schlafer goes on to say: "We do not need to hear nice words about what a happy day this is; how proud the parents must be; how honorable is the estate to which the candidate has been called. Nor do we need to hear a lecture about the baptismal covenant, the doctrine of the church, the nature of the vocational diaconate, or the liturgical functions reserved to the presbyterate. What we *do* need to hear on these occasions is God's clear, strong word to the church."[8]

That "clear, strong word" can be found in any number of Scripture texts that reveal what it means to be the church, the "called out," the *ekklesia*, who represent the presence of God's kingdom on earth. The preacher can explore ways in which this particular group of people under this particular leader in this particular time and place together can live into their Christian vocations. Through an occasion prompted by the recognition of one who will serve as a leader of God's people, the preacher can invite the community to think about what it means to do the following:

- worship the Lord with gladness and thanksgiving (Ps 100)
- comfort God's people (Isa 40)
- do justice and love kindness and walk humbly with God (Micah 6:6–8)
- serve those in need (Matt 25:31–46)
- wash one another's feet (John 13)
- pray and work for the unity of all who follow Jesus (John 17:6–26)
- feed Jesus's sheep (John 21:15–19)

- be marked as true Christians (Rom 12:9–21)
- proclaim Christ crucified in our words and deeds (1 Cor 1:18–31)
- imitate Christ's humility (Phil 2:1–11)
- live as a community of God's chosen ones (Col 3:12–17)
- be the church in a challenging world (Matt 5:10–12; Eph 6:10–20)

A song many of us learned as children in Sunday school declares, "*I* am the church; *you* are the church; *we* are the church together." That song expresses a simple yet profound truth about our common calling to be the body of Christ in and for the world. Celebrations of calls to ordained ministry are opportunities to recognize one whom God has "plucked up" from our midst. But they are also opportunities to remember that, as Paul reminded the church at Corinth, "neither the one who plants nor the one who waters is anything, but only God who gives the growth. The one who plants and the one who waters have a common purpose, . . . for we are God's servants, working together" (1 Cor 3:7–9).

Commissionings

If you pick up a worship bulletin or look at the website of any number of churches, you will see something like the heading "Pastors" followed by the names of the ordained staff and another heading that says "Ministers: All members of the church." That designation is a good reminder of our "common purpose" as "God's servants," as described in the text from 1 Corinthians 3:7–9 quoted above. But just as some of the baptized are called to ordained leadership in the church, others are called to specific ministries that serve the missions of congregations and church-related organizations. And those ministries are essential to the church's functioning, as anyone who has spent much time around churches will agree. Even those of us who have served as pastors will readily admit that most of the church's work is done not by the ordained or professional staff but by members of the congregation.

What Is Going On?

The doctrine of the "ministry of the laity" recognizes that those who have not been called to ordained leadership in the church live out their Christian vocations and use their God-given gifts in a variety of arenas. What is going on, then, when the church gathers to commission particular members for particular responsibilities is an acknowledgment that the church's work requires many individuals and a variety of gifts. Through services of commissioning, we celebrate those individuals and their gifts and, by the grace of God and the power of the Holy Spirit, consecrate them for special service. We give thanks for those who are willing to serve and what they bring to the shared life of the church. We also pledge our support and encouragement as the community of faith, the soil in which their gifts have grown and will continue to flourish.

Since services of commissioning embrace a variety of church workers and tasks, the focus of a particular service will be determined in large part by the individuals and ministries being recognized. Those workers and tasks include the following:

- church leaders and committee and board members (for both short- and long-term service)[9]

- teachers (of church school classes, youth groups, church-sponsored schools, after-school programs, and vacation Bible school)
- lay pastors and preachers and educators (who may be commissioned to serve a particular congregation or a group of churches)
- lay pastoral care providers (such as Stephen Ministers and hospice chaplains)
- groups undertaking mission and service projects (such as building a Habitat for Humanity house, working with refugee resettlement, or establishing a food pantry)
- church staff (including musicians and administrative and support staff)

Who Is Listening?

When we commission and bless church workers, those listening primarily will be the individuals called to service and the members of the congregation or other organization in which (or on behalf of which) they will serve. Most of those commissioned will be representatives of the congregation, known and even beloved in that community of faith. No matter the ministries being celebrated, those being commissioned and the community that commissions them come to worship with gratitude to God for the gifts and graces to be used for ministry in various ways. As with ordinations, some in attendance will bring feelings of pride in having nurtured those who have grown to the point of accepting a role in the ministry of the church.

But along with celebratory emotions, some will bring to services of commissioning a degree of anxiety about what their commitment entails and whether they will be able to live up to the responsibility. Teachers might wonder if their teaching will be effective. Stephen Ministers and pastoral caregivers might fear the emotional weight of their ministries. Those who undertake mission projects might wonder if they can handle the hard, physical labor involved. Board and committee members might worry about the time and energy required for their work and situations of conflict they might encounter. Some in the congregation might be fearful of potential changes in church traditions instituted by new staff or board members or even a new pastor selected by a search committee. Others will wonder if a new church school class or outreach program will succeed. But all will be eager to seek God's blessing upon the work of planting and harvesting that will continue through the ministries of the commissioned servants.

Where Is God?

We see God amid the mixed emotions present when we commission members for service to the church. God surely is in the call to an individual to accept a special task in or on behalf of a community of faith. God is in the gifts granted to individuals to do the work of the church and in their willingness to share those gifts. God is in the communities that nurtured those who have accepted positions of leadership and service. God is in the vision of a better future for the congregation, community, and world served by those who participate in the mission and ministry of the church.

Many of the texts suggested for ordinations are appropriate for services of commissioning as well. A number of other New Testament texts depict life in a Christian community as we accept various responsibilities and work together in mission to the world:

Matthew 28:16-20 The Great Commission.

John 15:12-17 Jesus has chosen us and appointed us to go and bear fruit and to demonstrate our faithfulness by loving one another.

Acts 2:43-47 Life among the believers.

Acts 6:1-6 The appointment of members of the community for various kinds of service.

Romans 12:1-8 Gifts that differ according to the grace given to us.

1 Corinthians 12 A variety of gifts are given to us by the Spirit to do the work of the body of Christ.

Ephesians 4:11-16 How Christ equips the saints for the work of ministry.

1 Peter 4:10-11 Serving God through the gifts we have been given.

Whenever we gather for worship as the people of God, we engage in "liturgy"—*leitourgia*—literally, the "work of the people." That "work" goes on beyond the pronouncement of the benediction at the end of the service, as members of the congregation live into their baptismal callings and carry out specific responsibilities for the mission of the church. It is appropriate that those workers are recognized and blessed by the people among whom and with whom they will plant and harvest as "servants of Christ and stewards of God's mysteries" (1 Cor 4:1).

Commitments

Ordinations to ministry and commissionings to specific tasks within and beyond the congregation are moments when we make promises as the baptized people of God. Other moments, however, evoke promises but in a more general way as we commit our lives and resources to the work of God through the witness of the church. We commit our lives when we are welcomed into a congregation as confirmands or new members. We commit our resources when we dedicate financial gifts and material goods, such as buildings and furnishings. We commit to God's ongoing work in the world through the founding of new congregations. We recommit to established ministries on the occasions of church anniversaries and homecomings.

What Is Going On?

When we celebrate commitments, what is going on is the community's recognition that God's work of planting and harvesting requires more than just good intentions. It requires an investment—an offering—of all that we are and have. Celebrations of confirmation or the reception of new members ask individuals to offer themselves to the work of a congregation and the mission of God in the world. Other services of commitment mark the offering of monetary resources by members and friends of the congregation to fund the work of the church that occurs by means of buildings, liturgical furnishings, personnel, programs, and outreach efforts. Still other occasions such as anniversaries and homecomings honor the witness of those who served and continue to serve an established church. And dedications of new buildings and the planting of new congregations represent investments in the future of the church by those who do the building and planting.

Who Is Listening?

On these special days, the listeners gathered will vary greatly depending on the reason for the service of worship and the people involved. Since most of these celebrations are acknowledged during Sunday morning worship, members of the congregation will compose the majority of the listeners who witness or make commitments to the ongoing work of a particular church. The congregation will bring a spirit of joy and hopefulness as it welcomes new siblings into the family of faith through confirmation and the reception of new members. The listeners on those special days might also include family members and friends—of various or no church traditions—who have come to celebrate with those joining the church. The new members standing before God and the congregation will bring a similar spirit of joy and hopefulness. But like those called and commissioned for designated ministries of the church, they might also bring a degree of uncertainty as to what their commitment entails and whether they are able to fulfill it.

Homecomings and anniversaries are meant to gather present and former members of the congregation to celebrate commitments made in the past and to recommit to the church's future. The listeners will give thanks for what the church has meant to them and, perhaps, to their families as they were nurtured in faith and engaged in service to the community and world. They will want to hear the stories of the people and events that shaped the history of that congregation and to share memories that make them laugh or cry. Some listeners will remember a "golden age" of the church that might be long gone and has little hope of being restored. For them, the joy of sharing memories might be tempered by the realities of a congregation with a questionable future. For at least a day, however, those gathered will celebrate the years of planting and plucking up that shaped the legacy of the congregation.

Occasions that include the dedication of monetary gifts and pledges or of buildings and furnishings gather listeners who believe in the mission of a particular congregation and who desire to see that mission continue. They will gather with the hope that their gifts will be used wisely to provide for regular opportunities for worship, education, and fellowship; for the care of members of the congregation; and for missions to the community and world. Guests from other congregations, the community, and the wider church might be present for the dedication of new buildings or the inauguration of a new church development. All who gather to celebrate commitments will come with hope in their hearts and thanksgiving on their lips as they witness the ongoing work of God's kingdom through the ministry of the church.

Despite the joy and hopefulness of celebrations of commitment, some who gather for those special days will carry realistic concerns and perhaps even doubts. Will the confirmands and new members promising to be faithful members of the congregation truly make the work of the church a priority in their lives? Can a struggling congregation count on the monetary gifts promised to come through to meet next year's budget? Will a new church being planted by representatives of a congregation or judicatory take root and develop? Does a church with a fruitful past have a realistic future in a changing neighborhood and world?

Where Is God?

Both the joys and uncertainties evoked by moments of commitment in the life of the church move us to wonder where God is present and at work on such occasions. Our faith, as witnessed in the work of the generations who have served the church before us and in the words of Scripture, assures us that God is the source of our gifts and abilities.

God enables us to make and keep our commitments. Whether we are pledging our time and energy or monetary and other tangible gifts, we quickly realize that the promises we make are not always easily kept. Our human frailty and fallibility too often thwart our best intentions. Scripture reminds us that we do not need to rely on our own limited power as we try to keep our commitments. We are instead upheld by the omnipotence of God as we engage in God's work in the world, as promised in texts such as these:

John 15:16	God will give us whatever we ask in Jesus's name.
Galatians 6:9–10	We do not give up as we work for the good of all, especially for those of the family of faith.
Ephesians 3:20	God's power within us is able to accomplish more than we can ask for or imagine.
Philippians 4:13	We can do all things through Christ who strengthens us.
2 Timothy 1:14	The Holy Spirit helps us guard the treasure entrusted to us.
Hebrews 12:1–3	We run the race set before us following the example of Christ.

God enables us to cultivate generosity in response to all that we have been given. "We give thee but thine own, what-e'er the gift may be" is a phrase from a hymn familiar to many congregations. It reminds us that we are stewards rather than owners of all that we are and have. That reminder can mitigate some of the dread with which preachers often face "stewardship Sunday." Regarding our financial commitments as our response to God's goodness helps us see our relationship with God as one in which we are totally dependent on God's grace. It also challenges us to think of stewardship as a daily, lifelong expression of our gratitude to God rather than as a day or season. Scripture confirms God's provision of abundance that can be shared:

> **Psalm 84:11** The Lord withholds nothing from those who walk uprightly.
>
> **Psalm 85:12** The Lord will give us what is good.
>
> **Psalm 103:5** God satisfies us with good as long as we live.
>
> **2 Corinthians 9:8–9** God blesses us with more than enough to share with others.
>
> **James 1:17** Every generous act of giving and every perfect gift is from God.

God enables us to work toward a future we might not see. An old Indian proverb says, "Blessed is he who plants trees under whose shade he will never sit."[10] That captures well the often-frustrating work of planting and plucking up that characterizes the ministry of the church. In God's infinite mercy and by means of the gifts we offer, the seeds we plant are nourished and grow. We are not always present for the harvest, however. But that reality does not prevent us from doing the work of cultivation. We continue to teach and preach, to care for one another and all of God's creation, and to proclaim God's kingdom yet to come. By the grace of God, we can see beyond the present work of planting to a future harvest of good things, encouraged by the words of Scripture:

1 Chronicles 22   David prepares to build God's temple, which he will never see.

1 Corinthians 3:10   By God's grace, we lay the foundation that others will build upon.

Philippians 1:6   The good work God began among us will come to completion by the day of Jesus Christ.

Hebrews 11:1–3   "Faith is the assurance of things hoped for, the conviction of things not seen."

Additional texts might be used for services of commitment.

Psalm 90:1–2   The Lord has been our dwelling place in all generations (for anniversaries and homecomings).

Psalm 90:17   The favor of the Lord will prosper the work of our hands (for the dedication of tangible gifts).

Psalm 127:1   "Unless the Lord builds the house, those who build it labor in vain" (for the dedication of new buildings).

2 Corinthians 8:1–7   God's grace enables us to excel in generosity (for stewardship).

1 Timothy 4:12   "Let no one despise your youth" (for confirmation).

Those of us who cherish the church and our vocations within it are well aware of the challenges we face as we try to hold fast to faith "in an age of change and doubt," in the words of Fred Pratt Green from a hymn many of us use to open worship. That same hymn, however, assures us that "God is here," amid the church's worship and work as we plant the seeds of the gospel and harvest the results of God's work through us. The church, it is comforting to remember, belongs not to *us* but to *God*, and even "the gates of Hades will not prevail against it," as Jesus declared (Matt 16:18). Every time a new minister or ruling elder or deacon is ordained, or a Sunday school teacher is commissioned, or a teenager is confirmed, or pledged gifts are dedicated, or ground is broken for a new church building, we say a defiant yes to God's ongoing work in the face of the world's indifference. And like the sower in Jesus's parable, who cast seed onto the ground, we stand in awe of the ways in which God blesses our meager efforts to plant the seeds of God's kingdom on earth, enabling those seeds to take root and produce a harvest of righteousness.

CHAPTER 5

Congregational Conflicts, Closures, and Changes

Donna Giver-Johnston

A time to break down, and a time to build up.
—ECCLESIASTES 3:3

I remember a retreat I led with the session of elders for a church I was serving at the time. I introduced the theme of the retreat by reading from Paul's first letter to the church in Corinth: "For just as the body is one and has many members, and all the members of the body, though many, are one body, so it is with Christ" (1 Cor 12:12). Then I continued, "If the ear would say, 'Because I am not an eye, I do not belong to the body,' that would not make it any less a part of the body. If the whole body were an eye, where would the hearing be?" (vv. 16–17). I asked people to share the body part with which they identified most based on their spiritual gifts. Some said their ears, others said eyes; some said hands, others feet, and a mouth for one who admitted she had the gift of gab. We all laughed knowingly. Then I read, "God has so arranged the body, giving the greater honor to the inferior member, that there may be no dissension within the body, but the members may have the same care for one another. If one member suffers, all suffer together with it; if one member is honored, all rejoice together with it" (vv. 24–26). I ended with Paul's final words of call and challenge: "You are the body of Christ and individually members of it" (v. 27). "How then," I posed, "do we work together as the body of Christ?" I paired together the ear and the mouth, the eyes and the feet, the head and the heart. They found it challenging to appreciate how their partners' gifts were just as valuable as their own. They practiced honoring each of the individual parts for the good of the whole body. We talked and listened. We laughed and learned. We bonded and became united in mission. Retreats are good for that. Once back at the church, our deeper appreciation of how our individual gifts work together for the common good continued to guide us and unite us in mission. Over time, we became a stronger church and a healthier body of Christ. That was then. Years after I left, I heard that this church was in crisis. The sense of unity broke down. It went through a time of conflict and division and dwindling membership. Today, it is healing and growing and reimagining life together as the body of Christ.

This is a familiar story. Many churches go through conflict, and all churches go through change. Some of the stories end with church closures; other stories involve seasons of change that lead to times of transformation and restoration. The fact is that in the life of the church, often there is a time to break down and a time to build up. During tumultuous times in the life of the church, in which the pastor is often involved, still people come to church needing to hear a word from God. This chapter will examine circumstances and occurrences of church conflict, closure, and change—seeking to understand what is going on, who is listening, and where God is—with the goal of finding a hopeful word to preach in times of congregational challenges.

What Is Going On?

"There's an elephant in the room" is an idiom used to describe an important topic or controversial issue that everyone is aware of but no one wants to talk about because it might make people feel uncomfortable, embarrassed, or angry. However misguided, people's intentions are good in ignoring the elephant. Every church has had such an elephant in the room at one time. It goes by many names: the beloved pastor left, a suspicious fire burned down the church, an elder's sexual misconduct was exposed, the treasurer was found guilty of financial embezzlement, a split occurred between those who prefer traditional music and those who prefer contemporary, dwindling membership drained the endowment, and so forth. This elephant that visits every church at one time or another, if ignored, will continue to cast a shadow on the ministry and compromise the health of the church. Often, preachers are called to this unenviable job of preaching to a church with an elephant in the room. Therefore, the first question the preacher needs to ask—and answer—is "What is going on here?"

Conflict

Data collected in the United States reveal a disturbing trend of conflict in churches. According to the 2010 Faith Communities Today (FACT) study, "Almost two of every three congregations in 2010 had experienced conflict in at least one of four key areas [worship, finances, leadership, priorities] in the past five years. In a third of the congregations the conflict was serious enough that members left or withheld contributions, or a leader left."[1] In 2015, the FACT report found that "the overall level of conflict in congregations remains unsettlingly high."[2] These statistics are disturbing, revealing how conflict is played out in destructive ways in the church. In *When Christ's Body Is Broken: Anxiety, Identity, and Conflict in Congregations*, pastoral care professor Leanna Fuller argues that congregational conflict "has the potential to break up the body of Christ into smaller and smaller pieces. In an era when the mainstream Protestant church is already suffering serious declines in membership, it is crucial for congregations to find healthier ways of handling conflict so that continued fragmentation does not remain the only option."[3]

When conflict is intense, emotions are heated, and sides are taken, finding a way through can be difficult and demanding. But that is just what Fuller aims to do in her article "A Splinter, Then a Crack: Leadership in the Aftermath of Divisive Conflict." Based on a qualitative study she conducted in 2019 with a Protestant congregation in which there was a significant conflict that split the church between those people with more "conservative" views, who left to follow the pastor, and those people with more "liberal" views, who stayed, she discovered pain and woundedness and broken relationships. She reports that interviewees described the conflict as "ugly"; "vicious, mean, and nasty"; "horrible"; and even "a bloodletting." Several people "used the metaphor of divorce to describe what the church split had been like."[4] Given their vivid descriptions, Fuller understands this conflict as a traumatic event that engulfed and damaged the entire congregation. Sadly, the church broke down.

In *Crisis Preaching: Personal and Public*, homiletician Joseph Jeter Jr. offers two categories to help identify the elephant in the church: "*Interruptive* crises have an *external* origin. They come upon people unbidden and unexpected." An example is a fire burning down the church building. "*Eruptive* crises break out from within."[5] Such systemic issues can erupt from time to time, cause damage, and force change. An example is an elder whose bullying behavior is not called out and who continues to weaken the health of the system. Both kinds of crises can crush the hopes of the congregation for the future of the church. Sometimes, the crisis is two-dimensional. For example, a denomination votes to allow same-gender marriages (*interruptive*) but leaves it up to the local churches to choose their own practices, so a congregation is split in half, each side demonizing the other (*eruptive*). The pastor's undesirable job is not just to identify the origin of the conflict but then to stand in the aftermath with the congregation and lead them through it.

In *Transitions: Leading Churches through Change*, homiletician John McClure's essay "Preaching as a New Pastor in Times of Congregational Crisis" ends with a clarion call: "The role of preaching in the midst of congregational trauma and leadership transition cannot be underestimated. In many respects, the tone, style, and direction of leadership in all congregations are all set from the pulpit, and those matters are of utmost importance in congregations experiencing significant disequilibria."[6] In the midst of disequilibria, the preacher can help the congregation stand on the solid ground of Scripture texts that tell the stories of people who experienced interruptive and eruptive conflicts and still kept the faith. The words of the prophets, handed down for generations, continue to inspire a renewed vision of a peaceable kingdom on earth:

> The wolf shall live with the lamb,
>   the leopard shall lie down with the kid,
>   the calf and the lion and the fatling together,
>   and a little child shall lead them. (Isa 11:6)

In the midst of a conflict, experienced by people as "a time to break down," the preacher is called to echo the promise of Scripture that there is also "a time to build up." And this is precisely the time to trust in Jesus, who came to establish God's kingdom of peace on earth, to lead the way to peaceful resolution, preaching, "You have heard that it was said, 'You shall love your neighbor and hate your enemy.' But I say to you, Love your enemies and pray for those who persecute you" (Matt 5:43–44).

Closure

But sometimes it seems as if there is no fixing the broken-down church. In the United Church of Christ (UCC), research specialist Taylor Billings Russell reports, "From January 2019 through June 2020, twenty-nine congregations in the UCC concluded their ministries. From January 2012 through June 2020, a total of 246 congregations made the decision to end their ministries and pass on their mission legacy. To put this in perspective, on average since 2012 one UCC congregation closes every two weeks."[7] This trend is occurring not just in the UCC. In Pittsburgh, following the 2018 decision of the Catholic Diocese of Pittsburgh to merge its 188 parishes into 57, the news reported the closure of numerous churches. In 2021, within ten miles of the Presbyterian church where I serve, two other Presbyterian churches closed their doors.

What is going on when a church closes? It is a painful process in which the pastor and remaining congregational members often feel guilty, wondering what more they could have done. The truth is that often, church closures have less to do with individual church's ministries and more to do with the cultural trends in our country today. According to the Faith Communities Report of 2020, "A similar pattern of fewer congregations growing plus rising percentages of those in decline can be seen across the decades of surveys." The data illustrate that in 2000, 20 percent of congregations were in decline, but in 2020, that number increased to 52 percent. In 2000, 53 percent of congregations reported growth of 5 percent or more; in 2020, only 34 percent of churches reported growth.[8] In "U.S. Church Membership Falls Below Majority for First Time," Jeffrey M. Jones reports, "Americans' membership in houses of worship continued to decline last year, dropping below 50% for the first time in Gallup's eight-decade trend. In 2020, 47% of Americans said they belonged to a church, synagogue, or mosque, down from 50% in 2018 and 70% in 1999."[9] From this data, we can clearly see that it is not just individual churches but religious institutions in general that have broken down.

But knowing they are in good company does not help ease people's pain about their own church's closure. Recently, a woman who belonged to a nearby church that has closed came to visit our church. She told me she was baptized in her church as a baby and had been worshipping there all eighty-four years of her life. She said as much as she appreciated our worship, she is just not ready to join another church. Reading between the lines, I wondered if she felt sadness that people drifted away, confusion over why they did, maybe some anger that the pastor did not do more to bring people in, and puzzlement over what more she could have done to save her beloved church. Sensing her palpable grief, I told her to take her time. For everything there is a season.

A pastoral leader who can frame the situation in broader terms than "If only we had served better coffee or allowed drums in our sanctuary" can help the faithful remnant to move from guilt to grace. In *Ending with Hope: A Resource for Closing Congregations*, editor Beth Ann Gaede presents wisdom from pastors who have shepherded their congregations through closing churches. From the beginning, Gaede frames the work in an important way: "We hope to help congregational leaders and supporters understand that closing a congregation is not about failure." In fact, all of the pastors who contribute to this volume share the belief "that closing a congregation is a resurrection opportunity to release resources for new ministry."[10] Closing a congregation is an opportunity for the pastor to preach with compassion the sermon Jesus preached, "Blessed are those who mourn, for they will be comforted" (Matt 5:4). And furthermore, it is an opportunity to preach with conviction the scriptural truth, "If we live, we live to the Lord, and if we die, we die to the Lord; so then, whether we live or whether we die, we are the Lord's" (Rom 14:8). In the life of a church, there is a time to build up and a time to break down. As preachers, we hold on to the promise and help our congregations hold on to the hope that God has made everything suitable for its time.

Change

On the morning of Sunday, March 15, 2020, I went to church to preach as usual. But there was nothing usual about this Sunday. The church building was closed due to the Covid-19 pandemic. The sanctuary was empty. The worship would be virtual. Thankfully, our church had been livestreaming our worship for two years, mainly for a few folks out of town or sick at home or in the hospital. But we still had much to change. We had to learn how to do Bible study using video conferencing. We had to learn how to encourage one another through daily emails with inspiring messages. We had to learn how to do ministry from a distance (e.g., sewing masks at home). I had to learn how to preach to empty pews. We all had to learn how to stay connected while staying apart. A colossal challenge, indeed, but knowing that we were not the only church facing this challenge helped us find the creativity and courage we needed not only to survive but to thrive. While most people grieved the loss of connection and community, others saw this as an opportunity to make much-needed changes in our congregation's use of technology to enhance our ministry and expand our outreach.

The 2020 FACT study reports a growing use of technology in churches, even in prepandemic times: "Although congregations were mostly slow to adopt internet tools, their use prior to the pandemic was growing significantly. Certainly, this trend has increased in the past 18 months. While having a website grew early and then leveled off, having a Facebook page has come to be nearly universally adopted as the congregational social media platform of choice."[11] The pandemic forced churches to adapt our ministries to meet the needs of people in a changing world. It was difficult, but possible and even rewarding. One Sunday after I preached on our ongoing connection and communion as the body of Christ and celebrated the sacrament during our livestream worship service, we met online to share communion with one another. Each person shared what bread they were eating. As I listened to a woman talk about the loaf of challah bread she had baked and saw the joy in the eyes of a young boy who got to have a juice box in the morning, I realized we were on holy ground. The congregation was divided into boxes on a computer screen, but still we were united as the body of Christ, very much alive!

Some changes—for example, a new Sunday school curriculum, a different worship service time, or a new and hopefully improved coffee for fellowship—are expected or subtle and easy to navigate. Other changes—members leaving to join the new church in town, new screens being installed in the sanctuary, or the death of a longtime pastor—are radical twists and turns that force a congregation toward an unwelcome shift, leaving them feeling anxious about the road ahead. These times in between the comfortable place we knew and the unknown place we are going can throw us off balance unless we, like Abraham, can step out in faith, trusting in the grace that will surely be revealed and accompany us on the way. Beverly A. Thompson and George B. Thompson Jr. wrote *Grace for the Journey: Practices and Possibilities for In-between Times* for pastors who are leading churches through change: "Our goal is to help you reframe this in-between time as sacred space when your congregation can rediscover its energy and witness."[12] The challenge for pastors is that often, we are leading our congregations through a time of grief and anxiety in the midst of our own uncertainty about the future. How is it possible to lead transformative change? First, we pray, "God, grant me the serenity to accept the things I cannot change, the courage to change the things I can, and the wisdom to know the difference."[13] Second, we preach words that are trustworthy and true: "Jesus Christ is the same yesterday and today and forever" (Heb 13:8).

Who Is Listening?

"There's an elephant in the room"—that is what is going on. Some people do not want to talk about it, but some do. Most people do not want to talk about it themselves but desperately want—or need—the preacher to do so. After we have understood what is going on in a challenging time in the church, before we can preach, we need to ask ourselves, "Who is listening?" People in a church that is conflicted, closing, or changing experience a range of emotions, including anger and anxiety, guilt and grief, frustration and fear, helplessness and hopelessness. In the midst of brokenness and pain within the body of Christ, people come to church with open wounds. They need to be seen and heard and healed. Some may come wanting to prove that "we were right" and "they were wrong." Others may come not knowing what happened. Still others come just wanting some peace. Everyone comes wondering where God is in this. As people come to realize that we cannot go back to the way things were and the way forward is unfamiliar and the destination uncertain, feelings of disillusionment can set in. This can be a difficult season, notes Leanna Fuller: "From a spiritual perspective, disillusionment might also include changes in individuals' or communities' understandings of God. Some may begin to question the nature of God's activity in or intentions for the world. Others will experience spiritual challenges such as disconnection, isolation, or a struggle to find meaning."[14] Together, these feelings can build on others and can take on the proportions of a giant elephant in the room.

Even if it's hard to hear, people desperately want someone to say, "There's an elephant in the room and its name is Anxiety or Grief or Disillusionment or Hopelessness." Once people recognize the elephant, claim their feelings, then and only then can the healing begin. This is the hard and holy work of a preacher who is called both to ask the question, "In light of this particular crisis, is there a word from the Lord?" and then to answer in no uncertain terms, "Yes, there is." Even if the preacher's knees are knocking behind the pulpit, she needs to speak the truth the people need to hear. Even if the preacher is intimidated by the naysayers, he needs to speak the truth and call the elephant by name. Even if the preacher is anxious, they need to speak the truth that God is at work even in these challenging times. For only this truth has the power to set the congregation free.

I will never forget the time that my church's choir director resigned and chose not to come to church on Sunday to say goodbye to the congregation. News began to spread, and people began to get anxious. My phone rang, and questions were asked and accusations made. Wondering if this would create a conflict in the church, I prayed fervently, "Is there a word from you, O Lord?" Thankfully I heard one, and with a small amount of courage and a huge amount of grace, I preached it that Sunday. Several people said to me that they did not want to come to worship because of their feelings of confusion, anger, disillusionment, and fear the church was falling apart. But afterward, they said they were glad they came to experience the power of the liturgy, the congregational prayer and singing, and my sermon, in which they heard a word from the Lord that reassured them God is with us and we will be all right. With courageous preaching, from times of conflict and anxiety can come positive changes of renewed faith and recommitted mission.

Confusion in the church has a long history—and so does courageous preaching. At Pentecost, the Holy Spirit appeared as divided tongues of fire. All the people who were speaking in different languages were amazed and perplexed, saying to one another, "What does this mean?" But others sneered and said, "They are filled with new wine" (Acts 2:12). Surrounded by people who were confused and concerned about the lack of good order, Peter stood up and raised his voice and preached,

"Listen to what I say" (Acts 2:14). People listened, the good news spread, and the church grew. The rest is history—living history! Inspired by the example of courageous preachers like Peter, we dare to preach sermons that are not afraid to name the elephant in the room as well as name the Spirit powerfully uniting people in one heart and mind. To anxious listeners, we dare to preach sermons like "The End of the World as We Know It" by preaching professor John McClure: "Deep inside, these days, many of us are experiencing the end of the world as we know it. And we are asking like the church did on that ascension day long ago, 'Now what? Is this the time? *Shouldn't* this be the time? The time of God's great restoration?' We wish for it. We long for it. We pray for it."[15]

Before I preach—no matter the season—I begin with a prayer: "Speak Lord, speak a word of truth. Speak a word of power. Speak Lord, for your people are listening." In times of congregational conflict, closure, and change, surely the people are listening for a word from the Lord.

Where Is God?

When preachers speak truthfully that "there's an elephant in the room" and then courageously call it by name, they can expect a response. Members of conflicted or closing congregations ask many questions: Who caused this? What do we do now? When will the pain stop? How will we pick up the broken pieces and go on? Why did this happen? But in the midst of any kind of change, the most important question people are asking and need an answer for is "Where is God?"

Congregations that are not hearing a reassuring answer to the question of God's presence will have a more difficult way through the challenging time. Pastoral care professor Leanna Fuller goes beyond describing the conflict of the church she studied to offering a way through it. In the interviews, one of the most important aspects of healing cited was the pastoral leadership. Fuller claims that pastoral leaders are charged with helping their communities understand conflicts in light of theology. She writes, "Pastoral leaders are called to invite the church as a whole to reimagine their narrative through the lens of faith."[16] She uses pastor and clinical counselor Lisa Maddox's term *restorying*, in which pastoral leaders help conflicted congregations move from "problem-saturated stories" to "hope-saturated stories."[17] Enter the preacher, who is called to interpret the word of God for the people of God, telling the story of our conflicted lives in light of the story of our covenanted faith, telling the story of our real losses in the light of God's radical love.

Preachers have a plentiful supply of hope-saturated stories in Scripture. Hope is what the prophets spoke to people when things were broken down. The prophet Isaiah said to the people exiled from their homeland,

> But now thus says the Lord,
>   he who created you, O Jacob,
>   he who formed you, O Israel:
> Do not fear, for I have redeemed you;
>   I have called you by name you are mine.
> When you pass through the waters, I will be with you;
>   and through the rivers, they shall not overwhelm
>   you;
> when you walk through fire you shall not be burned,
>   and the flame shall not consume you.
> For I am the Lord your God. (Isa 43:1–3)

Notice Isaiah does not say *if* but *when* "you pass through the waters." Times of challenge will come to all of us. But trusting that God will be with us, we can even walk through the fires of church challenges and not be burned. A spirit strengthened and sustained by this steadfast hope cannot be broken.

When the church is too broken, the people too despairing, the road to restoration too arduous, the pastor holds space for hope to be restored, praying with the apostle Paul "that with the eyes of your heart enlightened, you may know what is the hope to which he has called you" (Eph 1:18). Saint Augustine is believed to have said, "Hope has two beautiful daughters; their names are Anger and Courage. Anger at the way things are, and Courage to see that they do not remain as they are." In the face of congregational crises, in order to have sure and steadfast hope, pastoral leaders need to befriend Hope's two daughters. We pastors need not be afraid of Anger but should be righteously indignant about the way things are on behalf of our broken congregations. At the same time, we need to get to know Courage to help us step up and speak out and lead in the way of healing and wholeness.

In *Quietly Courageous: Leading the Church in a Changing World*, former Alban Institute consultant Gil Rendle claims, "The meaning of faith cannot be delivered by a weak story of loss and decline. An honest picture of the current reality along with a real hope for a better future are the two sides of the most critical aspect of leadership . . . the building of a new and better narrative for people to live."[18] One way Rendle encourages this building of a new and better narrative for people to live is through curiosity, by inviting the congregation to reflect on questions such as "Who are we, now? Who is our neighbor, now? What does God call us to do, now? How will we do it? What have we learned about our experience? What reshaping or changing do we need to work on because of what we have learned?"[19] Preachers can ask these questions of Scripture texts on behalf of the congregation, in sermons sharing their pastoral insights of real hope for a better future.

"Hope arises from our doubts, dilemmas, quandaries, and failures," argues Rendle. "Hope does not prevent or escape them but is built on what we learn from them." From his personal experience of suffering, the apostle Paul encourages the church in Rome: "We also boast in our sufferings, knowing that suffering produces endurance, and endurance produces character, and character produces hope, and hope does not disappoint us, because God's love has been poured into our hearts through the Holy Spirit that has been given to us" (Rom 5:3–5).

The pastor of the conflicted church Fuller studied, whom she calls "Rev. Smith," acknowledged the hurt while also holding up hope for a fresh future for their faith community. Fuller writes, "Rev. Smith would often use the phrase 'It's a new day!' to remind parishioners that First Church did not have to be defined solely by the painful conflict it had endured."[20] Smith's claim of hope is rooted in the Bible. Because the psalmist once testified, "This is the day that the Lord has made. Let us rejoice and be glad in it" (Ps 118:24), Rev. Smith can proclaim the truth, "It's a new day!" with steadfast hope that it will be so.

In this challenging time of the overall decline of the church in today's culture, pastors are called to the hard work of building up the body of Christ. We are called to be courageous leaders in our pastoral and pulpit ministries, which we cannot do without a rich prayer ministry. William Sloane Coffin, former senior minister of Riverside Church in New York City, wrote a powerful prayer called "A Prayer for the Church in These Times."

The line that struck me most was "Grant us to count our more complicated blessings: our failures, which teach us so much more than success."[21] Surely this is our call as preachers today: to help people count our more complicated blessings that present themselves as failures—congregational conflicts, closures, and changes—and to give thanks for them to God, from whom all blessings flow.

In challenging times in the church, congregations cry out for answers, for assurances that God has not abandoned them. Courageous pastors dare to call out the elephant in the church by name, but they also testify that we are not alone with an elephant in the room. "Is God with us?" we dare to ask. And then, we answer with an unequivocal yes, witnessing to the truth that nothing "will be able to separate us from the love of God in Christ Jesus our Lord" (Rom 8:39). We dare to preach sermons like John McClure's "The End of the World as We Know It," which ends with an assurance of God's presence and providence: "On this 'in-between day,' . . . Remember that God meets us at the end of the world as we know it—meets us with a vision of the beginning of the world as God knows it—of our humanity and our frailty and our suffering and our longing taken up into God's heart, transformed, and one day coming home for good."[22] Like McClure, we preachers are called to answer the question people anxiously ask, "Where is God?" with a courageous word: "God is with us." In the life of a church, there will always be a time to break down. And this is precisely the time for preachers to secure the hope that God has made everything suitable for its time. Even in troubling times, perhaps especially in complicated times that people will never forget, preachers are called to proclaim a word of hope that people will always remember: God is with us. God is with us in conflict, closure, and change. God is with us in anxiety, grief, and fear. From Emmanuel to Everlasting. God is with us. Evermore and evermore.

Preachers are called to stand with a congregation in times of conflict, closure, and change and, in such times as these, to courageously peach that in "a time to break down," we have steadfast hope that there is "a time to build up." For God has made everything suitable for its time. What then shall we say about these things? To find a word from the Lord, here are some suggested Scriptures for preaching in these troubled times:

To calm congregations in conflict

Psalm 42   "Why are you cast down, O my soul,
and why are you disquieted within me?
Hope in God; for I shall again praise him,
my help and my God."

Matthew 11:28–30   Jesus said, "Come to me, all you that are weary and are carrying heavy burdens, and I will give you rest."

Matthew 22:39b   Jesus said, "You shall love your neighbor as yourself."

Mark 4:35–41   In the midst of the storm, his disciples cried out, "'Teacher, do you not care that we are perishing?' [Jesus] woke up and rebuked the wind, and said to the sea, 'Peace! Be still!' Then the wind ceased, and there was a dead calm."

To comfort congregations closing their church

Joshua 1:9   "Be strong and courageous; do not be frightened or dismayed, for the Lord your God is with you wherever you go."

Ezekiel 37 "Thus says the Lord God to these bones: I will cause breath to enter you, and you shall live. . . . My dwelling place shall be with them; and I will be their God, and they shall be my people."

John 14:1–6 Jesus said, "Do not let your hearts be troubled. Believe in God, believe also in me. In my Father's house, there are many dwelling places. If it were not so, would I have told you that I go to prepare a place for you?"

Revelation 21:3–5 "See, the home of God is among
mortals.
He will dwell with them;
they will be his peoples,
and God himself will be with them;
he will wipe every tear from
their eyes.
Death will be no more;
mourning and crying and pain will be
no more."

To reassure congregations in times of change

Psalm 46:1–2, 7 "God is our refuge and strength,
a very present help in trouble.
Therefore we will not fear, though the
earth should change. . . .
The Lord of hosts is with us;
the God of Jacob is our refuge."

Isaiah 40:28–31 "Those who wait for the Lord shall renew
their strength,

they shall mount up with wings like
eagles,
they shall run and not be weary,
they shall walk and not faint."

Romans 8:25–28 "We know that all things work together
for good for those who love God, who are
called according to his purpose."

Hebrews 12:1–2 "Therefore, since we are surrounded by so
great a cloud of witnesses, let us also lay
aside every weight and the sin that clings
so closely, and let us run with perseverance
the race that is set before us, looking to
Jesus."

This list of biblical texts is provided to guide you in selecting
an appropriate scripture for preaching on occasions of church
conflict, closure, or change. In an interview with Sheldon Sorge
(general presbyter of Pittsburgh Presbytery) about preaching to
congregations in some form of distress, I learned that he favors
using the lectionary in order to avoid the temptation of choosing
a scripture to fit a situation, which can lead to preaching with a
"biblical arsenal to unload." Regardless of how the text is chosen,
he recommends a "perspectival approach," which uses Scripture
not as an object but as a lens through which to see particular
people struggling with a particular issue at a particular time.
In so doing, he is able to preach sermons that help people see their
situation with a fresh perspective that enables a faithful response.
Still, Sorge admits that in the many difficult times he has been
called to preach to churches, using many different lectionary
texts, he tends to preach a version of the same sermon—that
of reconciliation. Of any text—lectionary or self-selected—he

asks the same question: "In a polarized world or church, marked with acrimony and mistrust, what does it mean to be a community that in our life demonstrates the reconciliation of God's work through Jesus Christ?"[23] A preacher who is able to name the elephant in the room and witness to God's reconciling power through the word read and proclaimed can move people from problem-saturated stories to hope-saturated stories and, in so doing, help speed the healing of wounded people and the building up of the body of Christ.

"The Blind Men and the Elephant" is a parable from India that has been adapted by many religions and published in various stories for adults and children. It is about a group of blind men who attempt to learn what an elephant is, each touching a different part and disagreeing on their findings. One man touched the side and said the elephant was like a wall. Another man touched the trunk and said the elephant was like a snake. Another touched the ear and said the elephant was like a fan. Still another touched the tail and said the elephant was like a rope.[24] When an elephant is in the room of the church, people become anxious. In a time when the church seems broken, people quarrel over what is happening and where God is. Like the blind men in the parable, people think they can diagnose and solve the problem on their own. The truth is, it takes a courageous pastor and a committed congregation together, willing to step back and see the whole elephant for what it is—to name it and claim it as part of their story, as part of God's story. And the good news of God's story is that it does not end with a time to break down but with a time to build up—a time to raise Jesus up from the grave. In the resurrection, his body was raised up so that the church could be built up as the body of Christ on earth.

One Sunday, for our "Time with the Children," I led a game of "Simon Says." I said, "Simon says, 'Touch your head.'" Immediately, the children touched their heads. "Simon says, 'Touch your toes.'" The children giggled as they touched their toes. "Simon says, 'Touch the church.'" After an awkward silence, invariably, the children touched something in the chancel—the pulpit, the table, the font, or a step—whatever they could reach. I affirmed their touch, and then I talked about how the church is all those things and how the church is also the people in it. In fact, the church Jesus called was first and foremost the people. The Bible says that the church is "the body of Christ," and we are each and every one of us members of it (1 Cor 12:27). In my own words, I told the children how each one of us is a part of the church and that it takes all of us to be the church together. "Now let's try again," I said. "Simon says, 'Touch the church.'" The children touched someone sitting next to them. We sang together, "I am the church, you are the church, we are the church together. All who follow Jesus, all around the world, yes, we're the church together." After our prayer, as the children were on their way to Sunday school, I saw a young girl touch an adult in the pew, saying, "You are the church."

This story will preach! As a little child reminds us, the church is more than its problems. The church is more than broken. By the power of the resurrection, the church of Jesus Christ is being built up and raised up. The church is being renewed and reformed and made new, day by day, in amazing ways. Morning by morning, new mercies we see. It's a new day! May it be so.

CHAPTER 6

Older Adult Communities

Beverly Zink-Sawyer

A time to weep, and a time to laugh.
—ECCLESIASTES 3:4

On more Sunday afternoons than I could count, while I was a pastor, I found myself leading worship in a local facility for the elderly. I must confess that I did not always approach those responsibilities with a cheerful heart. After leading two worship services and often an educational event on Sunday morning—and facing the evening church events to come—I would close up my office, grab some lunch, and head off to a retirement community or nursing home somewhere across the county. The last thing I wanted to add to a busy Sunday schedule was another worship service for people I might not even know. But like so many surprising things that come our way in ministry, those services were often the highlight of my week. They provided opportunities for people who were cut off from the lives they once enjoyed to express their gratitude and faithfulness to God. And the spirit

I encountered among those gathered lifted my own heart and reminded me why I had answered the call to ministry.

Many seasons of our lives are marked by a mix of conflicting emotions. The Ecclesiastes preacher must have realized that and so gave us this series of antithetical couplets. One of the most obvious seasons of mixed emotions is that of the later years of life. Most (although, admittedly, not all) people have much for which to be grateful in old age. Lives that have been rich in blessings and full of accomplishments can be celebrated. Wisdom, as often expressed in the Old Testament, has been gained and can be shared. Good memories can be revisited. The later years of life are, for many, a time to look back and smile and laugh, even at the mistakes made along the way. At the same time, those years evoke much weeping: weeping over regrets that continue to haunt us, lost loved ones and opportunities, and diminished strength and abilities. Preachers can speak to that range of emotions, offering comfort for those who weep and an invitation to celebrate for those still able to laugh.[1]

What Is Going On?

Few parish ministers will not encounter elderly listeners in their ministries. They may serve aging congregations, but even if they do not, they will likely be called upon to lead worship at local nursing homes and retirement communities. Many of those facilities, especially large ones and those that are sponsored by a religious denomination, will have their own or on-call chaplains. But they often invite local clergy to lead services so the residents can hear a variety of preachers representing different religious traditions and worship styles. The services are usually held on Sunday afternoons or evenings and are meant to provide opportunities for worship for residents who cannot attend local churches. Preachers may be invited to preside at special services for the facility at other times, such as Memorial Day or All Saints' Day (perhaps including the memorializing of community members who have died during the past year) or a memorial service for a church member who resided at the facility. For the most part, however, the services local clergy are invited to lead are intended to function like regular Sunday services.

While the services resemble typical Sunday morning worship services, those gatherings present the preacher with challenges. Like other occasions that occur outside the walls of the church, the space in which the worship service occurs can be problematic. The "sanctuary" provided in elder care facilities can be anything from a formal chapel to a cluttered activity room. The preacher might have to compete with the commotion of folks gathering with wheelchairs and walkers, loud television programs, ongoing meals, and other activities. The creation of "sacred space" by means of visual liturgical symbols is especially critical as both preacher and congregation enter into a holy moment in the presence of God.[2] Envisioning the space and perhaps even visiting it beforehand, if possible, can help the preacher think about ways to make the secular sacred. To the extent that the gathered worshippers can participate, hymns and even responsive readings and prayers can help shape the worship service. The important thing is that we find ways to bring our listeners into a holy, special place that allows them to worship in their own ways as they are able and to hear a comforting message from the Lord.

Who Is Listening?

When thinking about older adults, as with any generational cohort, it is too easy to assume that they are a monolithic group of listeners. With people living considerably longer than those in any previous generation, the assumptions we once made about old age are constantly being challenged. Gerontologists now divide the "elderly" into various stages and conditions within those stages—generally, the "young old," "middle old," and "old old." Even those designations, while somewhat helpful and indicative of general trends in the population, are challenged by many exceptions. In addition to diverse physical and mental conditions, any group of older listeners will represent a variety of life experiences, family circumstances, socioeconomic conditions, and political and religious beliefs. Thus, the first thing we as preachers need to acknowledge is that a group of older adults probably will be as diverse as any other group of people we address.

That said, elderly listeners share many of the same concerns. Primary among those concerns is the reality that their days are "numbered," to use the biblical term, and they have more past days to remember than future days to imagine. Gerontologists and others who work with elders understand meaning making to be the primary developmental task of late life. That task often results in a "life review," thinking back over their life experiences to make peace with regrets and celebrate accomplishments. They are often concerned about the various dimensions of the legacy they will leave behind. Some will think about their tangible legacies in the form of money and possessions. Others will wonder about how they will be remembered for raising their families, doing their jobs, and serving their communities. Still others will ponder their "spiritual legacies," as a chaplain friend of mine describes it: the ways in which their examples of faithfulness touched the lives and even shaped the faith of others. All of us as we age engage in such reflection, whether consciously or subconsciously, seeking ways to make sense of the past and find hope for the future. It invites us to weep over memories that still cause pain and laugh at those that still evoke joy.

In recognizing that their days are numbered, our elderly listeners share another universal concern: the inevitability of their own mortality. "Living" means something entirely different to those faced with the nearness of dying. Some elderly listeners will have made peace with the reality of death; others will not be willing to "go gentle into that good night," as the poet Dylan Thomas put it. Since people age so differently, some will be fully engaged in the activities of life to the best of their abilities and for as long as possible; others will have surrendered to the limitations of their aging and rest content to fade away. Regardless of one's beliefs about life after death, it is hard to avoid feeling some fear when facing the end of earthly life—and often that fear is less about death itself than what might precede it. The fear of a painful death or a lonely death or a death preceded by a long illness consumes the thoughts of many aging listeners. Being aware of and honoring these different approaches to the end of life is important as we think about what to preach.

In addition to that ultimate existential fear of death, few elderly listeners can escape everyday fears. Many carry financial fears, especially in the face of skyrocketing costs for health and long-term care in addition to monthly bills. Others worry about the quality of care they receive. They might also fear they will be neglected by their family, friends, and church or perhaps even abandoned in strange and lonely places. And like all of us, the elderly might be fearful of inevitable changes in their circumstances and the unknowns looming in the future.

The loss of life is but one of the many losses incurred as we age. In addition to facing that ultimate loss, elderly listeners encounter many smaller but still deep losses that wear them down and test their faith as they move toward death.[3] There are the obvious losses of physical and cognitive abilities that come to all of us as we age. Frail bodies and failing minds consume much of the attention of the elderly and cause their spheres of activity to shrink. The inability to do things they once enjoyed and took for granted is a cause for much weeping for those in their later years. They lose autonomy and control, handing over to others many of the decisions they once freely made. But those tangible physical and mental losses are exacerbated by other less obvious, but still painful, losses. They lose places once enjoyed, things once owned, people once loved, and identities once assumed. Many of our elderly listeners will be in living situations that are more necessary than chosen. They have relinquished homes and familiar communities. They may be physically distant from families and churches and social circles. They have had to "downsize" to a smaller home or apartment at best or one room at worst. As a result, loss and the grief it engenders become constant companions of the elderly.

With these thoughts about our elderly listeners in mind, other important considerations will enable us to preach to them effectively. Knowing the kind of older adult community we will be visiting and the extent and type of care offered there is essential in thinking about a sermon that will speak to those listeners. I have led worship services in continuing care communities where many of the worshippers present were retired professionals who had extraordinary careers and sharp, engaged minds. Some of the listeners were quite elderly, and others were what have been called the "young old," those in their sixties and seventies, but most of them remained healthy and active. The expectations of those listeners were high, and they were keen sermon critics! Others were simply attentive and grateful for an opportunity to worship.

The greater challenge for the preacher comes when preaching to listeners with limited or diminished cognitive ability, such as those in health care units or nursing homes. The reality of preaching in such settings is that many (perhaps most) of the listeners will not be aware of what is going on. The "listeners" might appear to be doing very little listening. They might even be determined to "preach" in competition with the preacher, something I've experienced many times! Others will surely be nodding off or even snoring loudly. It can be disconcerting, to say the least, for the preacher—especially a less-experienced one—to deal with this cacophony. But we persevere, not knowing what might spark a moment of recognition and awareness, even of laughter, within a listener who seems otherwise disengaged. Sometimes a special service is held for residents with cognitive impairment, while at other times they join with residents who may have physical but no cognitive issues, leaving the preacher to figure out how to "pitch" the sermon in order to reach the greatest number of listeners.

Often added to the mix of cognitive abilities represented in older adult communities is a variety of religious beliefs and backgrounds, educational levels, ideological commitments, and perhaps even socioeconomic and racial identities. And if all that were not enough of a challenge for the preacher, family members or caregivers might be in attendance at the service.

How, then, can we think about preaching with elderly listeners in mind? We can begin by picturing our listeners not just as they are but as they once were and as who they continue to be: individuals created and loved by God—whose image, the *imago Dei*, is indelibly stamped on them—who have lived long and full lives filled with moments of joy and sorrow, of weeping and laughter. Many of them have traveled widely, read extensively, and done amazing and creative work. They have lived through wars and rumors of war, natural disasters, political and social unrest, and times of plenty and want. They have faced personal hardships of all kinds and experienced deep sorrow as well as great joy. But in the end, they survived whatever life cast upon them, meeting it all with strength and resilience.

Reminding them of that strength and resilience through biblical stories and historical examples inspires motivation for facing the future. If we use our "sacramental imaginations" as preachers to think about the people who will be sitting before us, we will soon discover a treasure trove of sermon material on which to draw. "Then the stories will flow," as priest and preacher Walter J. Burghardt asserts, "some humorous, some tearful—stories from the storehouse of the aging." If we consider their experiences, "the imagination will break loose," and we will find rich meaning not only in the spectacular "but in the simple tales that keep the past alive in the present."[4]

There are, of course, practical considerations to keep in mind as we preach for older adults. The worship space in the facility can affect how the preacher is seen and heard, but making as many necessary accommodations as we can is part of our pastoral duty. Even the best prepared, most eloquent sermon is rendered useless if it cannot be heard. We might be able to move a lectern to be closer to the people. If we are not tied to a manuscript or notes for our sermon, we might be able to move around through the gathered group. The personal connection between preacher and people through eye contact and body language is always essential for communicating the message but even more so for older listeners. We might take that connection even further by asking a few questions during the sermon to engage the listeners. And a final practical consideration in preaching for older adults is sermon length. Less is more in this preaching context, since many of our listeners will have diminished attention spans or may even be in some physical discomfort.

All of us, no matter our ages, find comfort in the familiar. This is even more the case as we age. Preachers who lead worship for elderly listeners will find that familiar stories, hymns, texts, and prayers will resonate with elderly listeners. Many times, I've had the experience of leading worship in nursing homes where the listeners were virtually unresponsive other than the occasional inappropriate outburst. But when I invited them to recite the twenty-third Psalm or to sing "Amazing Grace" or to pray the Lord's Prayer, many of them chimed in heartily. No matter the extent of cognitive impairment, familiar words heard often and memorized long ago come to mind once again. And I often see obvious expressions of joy as they become participants in worship once again if only for a passing moment. That said, many older listeners are eager to hear and learn something new. It might be new insights on an old, familiar story or text or simply a connection to a current event. We honor our listeners by both comforting them with what is familiar and challenging them with something new.

One final consideration for many preachers when preaching to older adults is the age difference between the preacher and the listeners. When I first began leading Sunday afternoon services in nursing homes and retirement communities, I was in my midtwenties and wasn't sure I had anything worthwhile to say to people several decades older. The folks who attended those services were tolerant and even appreciative of my efforts, even when I'm sure I badly missed the mark. Over time, however, I came to know some of those folks and many like them who were members of my own congregation. Listening to and learning from elderly members through visits and conversations—as well as experience with my own elderly relatives—helped me develop sensitivity to their perspectives. As with other listeners from whom we might feel distanced because of life circumstances or experience, we can relatively easily gain understanding of the elderly if we are willing to spend time engaging them in conversation and asking questions about their memories and dreams, their hopes and fears. We can engage the "sacramental imagination" mentioned earlier to see through the eyes of our older listeners as we prepare to preach.

Walter J. Burghardt quotes theologian Henri Nouwen, who states that "care for the elderly means, first of all, to make ourselves available to the experience of becoming old." Burghardt adds, "Once preachers have allowed the aging into their own lives, have opened themselves to the experience of aging (whatever their age), have listened as if their own lives are at stake (as they indeed are), then the actual preaching is far less fearsome."[5] We will discover that, no matter our ages or circumstances, we have more similarities than differences as children of God. When we allow the aging into our own lives, as preacher and professor Cynthia M. Campbell notes, we are led "into deeper reflection on both the goodness of life and the reality of grace. It can convince the preacher, and (we hope) the congregation, of the importance of each day of life and confirm the confidence that both present and future belong not to us but to God."[6]

Where Is God?

If, indeed, both present and future belong not to us but to God, preachers need to connect the experiences of those who are aging with the promises of Scripture to remind them how God continues to work in their lives. Old age is a season of life that evokes much weeping *and* laughter. The good news for preachers is that there is no shortage of sermon material as we think about preaching for listeners in the later stages of life. As already stated, elderly listeners bring with them rich memories of the past, significant struggles in the present, and honest fears about the future. By acknowledging the realities of life as we age and also proclaiming that we live always in the presence of God, we create space for both weeping and laughter. The seasons of life—the past, the present, and the future—provide a way to think about several theological concepts and biblical texts that might be the focus of our preaching for older adults and remind them that all our days "belong not to us but to God."[7]

God Sanctifies the Past

One of the unique characteristics of human beings is the ability to remember and reflect on the past. This can be good news, since it enables us to process experiences, build on things we have learned, and relive moments of pleasure and joy. It can also be bad news, since it sometimes keeps us from relinquishing painful memories that prevent our moving forward and inhibit future happiness. As stated earlier, we all engage in what has come to be called a "life review" as we age. We cannot help but recall moments from the past—those that make us weep and that make us laugh. As preachers, we can invite our listeners to weep freely over their regrets but also give thanks for the memories that cause them to smile, acknowledging that *all* those moments belong to God, who not only accepts the past in all its beauty and ugliness but sanctifies it—declares it holy—as well.

No matter what we've experienced in life, we all have much to weep over as we review our lives. Few if any people reach old age without some regrets over choices made or not made, opportunities taken or not taken, or words spoken or left unspoken. Those regrets may be accompanied by feelings of shame or even anger. As we think about preaching to those who carry regrets over the past that might cause them to weep, *acceptance, grace,* and *forgiveness* become essential theological concepts for our sermons. We can invite our listeners to bring to God their regrets and brokenness, reminding them that "the sacrifice acceptable to God is a broken spirit; a broken and contrite heart" (Ps 51:17). Acknowledging the brokenness that haunts us—brokenness we have caused as well as brokenness thrust upon us—and knowing we do not bear it alone are the beginning of healing.

Ultimate healing, of course, comes by means of the grace we receive through God's Word, who "became flesh and lived among us." "From his fullness," John's Gospel goes on, "we have all received, grace upon grace" (John 1:14, 16). In many texts in the New Testament, especially texts from the letters attributed to Paul and other leaders of the early church, we are reminded that grace abounds. Those texts often point to a contrast between the harshness of life lived under the mandates of law and the joy of life lived under the grace of Jesus Christ. God's "new covenant" as promised through the prophet Jeremiah has been realized in Christ, as the writer to the Hebrews reminds us, assuring us that God will "be merciful toward [our] iniquities" and "remember [our] sins no more" (Heb 8:12). We are freed from the baggage of the past that weighs us down as we move into whatever future lies before us. Our past mistakes not only "pass away" but are obliterated, freeing us from any sadness and regret that might hold us back. As we are assured in the second letter to the Corinthians, "If anyone is in Christ, there is a new creation; everything old has passed away; see, everything has become new" (2 Cor 5:17).

Even as we might have much to cause us to weep in the final season of life, the psalmist reminds us that "weeping may linger for the night, but joy comes in the morning" (Ps 30:5). Elderly listeners who sit before us have lived long—sometimes very long—and, hopefully, full and meaningful lives. Behind every person of advanced age is a lifetime of stories, experiences, and contributions to their family, friends, communities, and workplaces. Through our sermon illustrations and invitations to revisit moments from the past, preachers can help older listeners tap into the storehouse of memories that cause them to smile and even laugh. A sermon on a text that acknowledges and even celebrates the goodness of the past allows the listeners to see not just their present limitations but the many ways in which they have been blessed by God and have been used to bless others. Reminding them of the gifts they have offered to future generations and the ways in which they will continue to shape the lives they have touched is cause for celebration. A sermon on the theme of thanksgiving for the opportunities and people and moments of grace that have filled their lives may be greatly appreciated.

Texts such as Psalm 77 invite us to "call to mind the deeds of the Lord" and remember God's "wonders of old" (Ps 77:11). Many other psalms implore us to give thanks to God for God's mercy and faithfulness. Psalm 116 expresses thanksgiving for God's protection in the past and asks, "What shall I return to the

Lord for all his bounty to me?" (v. 12). Paul's closing words to Timothy speak for so many faithful elders who can say, "I have fought the good fight, I have finished the race, I have kept the faith" (2 Tim 4:7). Reminders of the presence of God throughout their lives not only offer older adults an opportunity to acknowledge and give thanks for what has been but provide them with the assurance that, just as God has been faithful to them in the years past, God will continue to be with them as they live into whatever lies ahead. The words of the treasured hymn "Amazing Grace" ring especially true among elderly listeners: "'Tis grace has brought me safe thus far, and grace will lead me home."

God Upholds Us through the Present

Naming the grace that "will lead [us] home" is especially important as we think about preaching to older adults. While memories of the past occupy their minds in many ways, it is the exigencies of the present that are of primary concern for them. As already stated, all elderly listeners have experienced various kinds and degrees of loss that weigh them down. Preachers must acknowledge those losses and the grief—the weeping—that accompanies them while reassuring their listeners that they do not face those losses alone. At the same time, we can encourage older listeners to persevere in their engagement with and activities in the worlds they now inhabit, pointing to places where they can still discover joy.

Many Scripture texts, most notably from the psalms and the prophet Isaiah, testify to our God, who bears us through times of trouble. Psalm 91 expresses a beautiful vision of God, who shelters us "under his wings" and commands the angels to guard us "in all [our] ways." Isaiah assures us that God's Suffering Servant, whom we see reflected in Christ, has "borne our griefs and carried our sorrows" (Isa 53:4 KJV). Also through the prophet Isaiah, we are reminded that when we "pass through the waters" of pain and sorrow, God will be with us. No rivers will overwhelm us, and fires will not consume or even burn us (Isa 43:2). And at a time of life when power and strength are lost or at least diminished, we are assured that "those who wait for the Lord shall renew their strength," enabling them to mount up with wings like eagles, run and not be weary, walk and not faint (Isa 40:31). What a powerful word for those who have become weakened by age! In the New Testament, Jesus promises his continued presence and strength through the Holy Spirit, the Advocate, the one who comforts us when our hearts are troubled (John 14). Because of the Spirit's presence, we know that nothing, neither the losses we might experience nor the isolation we might feel, "will be able to separate us from the love of God in Christ Jesus our Lord" (Rom 8:38).

Perhaps the most devastating change faced in the later years of life involves diminished strength and abilities. While God's comfort through those inevitable changes is an important theological concept to address when preaching for the elderly, we cannot forget to offer inspiration to our listeners to persevere in doing whatever they can do despite their limitations. Some listeners will still be able engage actively in ministries of the church or community as they had done faithfully in their earlier years, while others will be limited to supporting ongoing work with their resources and prayer. Preachers can also name and uphold the wisdom of age and suggest opportunities for sharing that wisdom through mentoring, conversations with younger people, writing about their experiences of life, and enjoying family and caregivers. We can point to biblical examples of faithfulness late in life as shown in the lives of Elizabeth and Zechariah (Luke 1) and Simeon and Anna (Luke 2). At the very least, we can encourage them to "devote [themselves] to prayer" (Col 4:2) for their own concerns, their loved ones, the church, and all the needs of the world, reminding them that, in the words of James, "the prayer of the righteous is powerful and effective" (Jas 5:16).

It is easy for our elderly listeners to miss the value of the present when consumed by regret over the past and worry about the future, but as Cynthia Campbell asserts, "*This* is the day God gives each of us. This is the only day we really 'have' in which to glorify and serve God and to begin enjoying God forever. . . . *This* is the day when we can respond to God's call and know God's affirming and redeeming presence."[8] To enable our listeners to recognize the gift of each day, no matter its hardships, and find some way to persevere and rejoice in it is the challenge—and the joy—of preaching to older adults.

God Offers Hope for the Future

Even as our older adult listeners find ways to persevere through present losses and rejoice in each day, they always face an unknown future. Some face that future with a sense of peace and acceptance; others face it with fear. For those who are fearful, preachers can name that fear and help their elderly listeners stare it in the face. Perhaps the psalms best address the fears that hold us captive later in life. "God is our refuge and strength, a very present help in trouble" (Ps 46:1) can be a comforting mantra for those who feel abandoned in the face of loneliness and weak in the face of illness. The next verse of that psalm, "Therefore we will not fear, though the earth should change," speaks to yet another emotion—the fear of change—that is the constant companion of so many in their later years. Other psalms, such as the beloved twenty-third Psalm, assure us of deliverance from our enemies, whether that enemy is illness, impending death, or isolation. As elderly listeners move into the unknown of the future, whether with contentment or fear, reminders of God's presence with the people of Israel as recorded in the stories of the Old Testament can offer a meaningful message. God commands Joshua to "be strong and courageous; do not be frightened or dismayed, for the Lord your God is with you wherever you go" (Josh 1:9). The assurance of divine presence is echoed in Jesus's postresurrection promise to the disciples—"I am with you always, to the end of the age" (Matt 28:20b)—and in Paul's question to the Romans: "If God is for us, who is against us?" (Rom 8:31).

The most significant fear of many who are aging is, of course, the fear of death and what might precede it. Preachers will want to acknowledge that "as all die in Adam," our faith nevertheless affirms that "all will be made alive in Christ" (1 Cor 15:22). Thus, the ultimate word of comfort we can offer to assuage the fears of those in their later years is the hope we have in God's saving work in Jesus Christ. A reminder that this is what our faith is all about is never more important than when addressing those facing the reality of death, as Episcopal priest Barbara Brown Taylor discovered when leading worship at a local nursing home. In an effort to create order amid the restive afternoon group of worshippers, she clapped her hands and asked them to choose the gospel lesson for the day: "'What shall I read from the Bible this afternoon?' I asked them. 'What part would you like to hear?' The commotion lessened long enough for one old woman's broken voice to be heard above it. 'Tell us a resurrection story,' she said. . . . 'Yes,' someone else said, and then someone else. 'Yes. Tell us a resurrection story.'"[9]

As preachers, we are always called to "tell a resurrection story," to name the grace of God that is the good news of the gospel. The good news that frail, often fearful folks nearing the end of life need to hear is that because of God's love for us in Christ and our faith in him, we "may not perish but may have eternal life" (John 3:16). Preachers can draw from the abundance of texts in which Christ himself and his earliest followers bear witness to that truth. We can also draw from our liturgical traditions, such as the memorial acclamation from the eucharistic prayer, which declares, "Christ has died; Christ is risen; Christ will come again." The "Witness to the Resurrection," as the funeral service is called in many traditions, reminds all of us, no matter our stage of life or nearness to death, of the sure and certain hope of the resurrection that is the central conviction of our Christian faith. It is because of God's promise of resurrection to new life that our weeping turns to laughter in the face of the challenges of life, including the ultimate challenge of death itself.

One thing we would do well to avoid when preaching to the elderly is a simplistic, "pie in the sky" kind of hope that ignores the painful realities many experience in the final years of life. As preachers, we can acknowledge and hold the losses, grief, and fears our listeners bring to worship while pointing to the ways in which God stands with us no matter what we face. We can also join them in leaning into the mystery that is God's promise of life beyond death. Even the apostle Paul confesses to a lack of understanding in his discourse on resurrection when he writes, "Listen, I will tell you a mystery! We will not all die, but we will all be changed" (1 Cor 15:51). Other texts mention "the mystery of Christ" (Col 4:3) and "the mystery of our religion" (1 Tim 3:16). As homiletician David Buttrick suggests,

"Along with the elderly, let us stand before the mystery of dying and, thereby, see into the mysteries of living."[10] Together with our listeners, we can see the vision of John that pictures a new heaven and a new earth where God dwells with us, destroying mourning and pain and even death itself, and wipes every tear from our eyes (Rev 21).

Additional scripture texts that speak to older adults

Psalm 71:17-20	God does not forsake us in our old age.
Psalm 90	God as our dwelling place through all generations.
Proverbs 16:31	Gray hair as a crown of glory.
Isaiah 46:3-4	God promises to carry us even when we turn gray.
Jeremiah 29:11	God has plans for our welfare.
Joel 2:28	Even old men shall dream dreams.
Zechariah 8:4-5	A vision of the old and young joyfully living together.
John 21:18	Being led by others in old age.
2 Corinthians 4:16-5:7	Walking by faith and not by sight.
2 Corinthians 12:9-10	Through Christ, we are made strong in our weakness.
Philippians 4:4-13	Finding contentment and strength to face all things.

Preaching to older adults is challenging, to be sure, but it is also one of the great privileges of ministry. To stand with those who have lived full, faithful lives and join them in moments of weeping and laughter before God, assuring them that "in life and in death we belong to God" is a gift of great measure.[11] "Just think," pastor and preacher William J. Carl Jr. reminds us, "of being able to help others embrace the wisdom God has granted them through the years for the good of all, to share the visions that will enable them to go on serving in a meaningful way, and to find the strength needful for each day. . . . That truly is preaching the gospel to and for a graying temple."[12]

CHAPTER 7

Holy Days and Holidays

Beverly Zink-Sawyer

A time to mourn, and a time to dance.

—ECCLESIASTES 3:4

Among the many things a minister entering a new congregation must discern is the calendar of days treasured by that community of faith. Sometimes we learn about their treasured days the hard way. Too many of us can recall regrettable experiences resulting from failing to give enough attention to Mother's Day, trying to exchange the party atmosphere of weekly potluck suppers during Lent for simple meals and contemplative services (my personal experience), or not including any patriotic hymns in the service on the Sunday closest to the Fourth of July.

Every congregational calendar is filled with days that mark the rhythm of the common life of that particular community. Some of those days are holy days, days that follow the liturgical calendar as it traces the life, death, resurrection, and ascension of Christ, whose work continues in the world. Other days are secular holidays that, by local practice, have become sacred in their own right for the congregations that celebrate them. While those days may be marked by one emotion or another—by the urge to dance or to mourn—some provoke a mix of feelings. The joy of national holidays characterized by gratitude and patriotism is tempered by recalling those who suffered and even gave their lives for our freedoms. The ashes of death that mark our observance of Ash Wednesday become the soil that births new life in the resurrection. The fire that ignited the first Christian communities on Pentecost is slowly being extinguished in our own time by apathy and secularism. By inviting listeners to both dance and mourn as we observe holy days and holidays, preachers can breathe new life into days that have grown too familiar.

"Biblical faith has always had a primary stake in the calendar," homiletician J. Ellsworth Kalas reminds us.[1] The narratives of the Old Testament mention specific periods of time: six days of work and one of rest in the story of creation, forty days and nights of rain upon Noah and his family, forty years of wandering the wilderness for the Israelites. In the New Testament, Jesus's temptation in the wilderness lasted forty days, and the hours of his agony on the cross were noted by the Gospel writers. The observance of Jewish festivals marked the life of Jesus and the rhythm of the early church until they were supplanted by Christian celebrations or infused with Christian meaning.

Something within our primordial DNA as human beings demands markers to define the passing of time. "We refuse to let time be a flat plain," Kalas observes. "We insist that it be marked by peaks of significance. Furthermore, we aren't satisfied with the peaks nature has built in; new moons and seasons aren't enough. So we raise up peaks of our own."[2] As people of faith, we are even more invested in the creation and observance of those peaks, for we believe we live "at the intersection of time and eternity," in the words of Laurence Hull Stookey noted earlier—in a continuum of history "in which God is perpetually at work in all of creation."[3] So Stookey asks, "Is it odd, then, that Christians find spiritual time-keeping to be so crucial to their identity and action?"[4]

While preaching the calendar enables individuals as well as congregations to mark time in their lives and strengthen their faith, significant challenges face the preacher when discerning how to address both holy days and holidays from the pulpit. When we think of major holy days such as Christmas and Easter, we wonder what more can be said after countless sermons over hundreds of years. When we think of major secular holidays and whether and how they should be addressed in the context of worship, we enter disputed territory, where we find Christians holding divided opinions regarding the separation of church and state. If we as preachers, however, are willing to invest the time and energy and prayer required to think through a special day by means of asking what is going on, who is listening, and where God is at work, we can bring our listeners into a holy space where we can mourn or dance together—and sometimes do both—in the presence of God. It is indeed, as Kalas declares, up to the preacher to make the most of important days: "In the case of sacred days, to be sure their sacredness is more fully comprehended by the people of God, and in the case of the secular, to invest them with the sacred potential that is their due."[5]

Holy Days

Among the gifts of the liturgical renewal movement that swept over many Christian traditions in the closing decades of the twentieth century is a greater emphasis on the liturgical calendar. All Christians celebrate the major festivals of Christmas and Easter and perhaps the seasons of Advent and Lent that precede them, but many of us grew up in Protestant churches (even mainstream ones) that ignored the lesser festival days. Recapturing the fullness of the Christian calendar provides a means to a deeper faith and a clearer understanding of God's continued presence and work among us. Holy days enable us to look "back to the future," to see the ways our God, who has been faithful in the past, will lead us in the days ahead. They provide teachable moments for individuals and communities seeking inspiration for living into the demands of Christian discipleship in a challenging world.

Each holy day has its own answers to the questions of what is going on, who is listening, and where God is at work, but a few generalizations about holy days can be made. What is going on is usually quite clear: a gathering for worship with a particular focus on the holy day. Most holy days occur on Sunday, making the celebration a part or even the focus of usual Sunday morning worship, often with special music, prayers, and liturgies. Some holy days, such as Ash Wednesday, Good Friday, and often All Saints' Day, occur on weekdays, creating reasons for special worship gatherings. Those who gather are, for the most part, from the usual Sunday morning congregation, perhaps with the addition of visitors who are moved to attend church on the major festival days. Regardless of their faithfulness to or familiarity with the church, we can assume that the listeners before us will want to hear how this special day relates to their lives. How does this day lighten the burdens they bear and deepen the gratitude they express for God's blessings? How does this day call forth the "cloud of witnesses" who have celebrated this day before us and now stand with us as we mourn and dance? What does this day offer us when juxtaposed with events unfolding around us in our community and world?

The good news about holy days is that they all are shaped by texts chosen to fit the day for lectionary-based traditions. Even holy days that occur on a day other than Sunday have stated Scripture readings. In addition, some days have been celebrated by the church for hundreds, even thousands of years, providing examples of how we can make the day meaningful for believers today. Preachers who ask where God is at work on holy days will find helpful answers in the ways special days have shaped communities of faith throughout Christian history. Resources recounting Christian practices surrounding holy days are abundant and readily available, making each holy day a "teachable moment."

Because there are too many days to address or even name here, and because every denomination (and every congregation) has its own calendar of holy days, I offer below some thoughts on a few days—days that have grown familiar and others that are less familiar that might strengthen the faith of listeners in new ways—to serve as examples of how preachers can "think through" a holy day to reach a meaningful message. The process of thinking about what is going on this day, who might be listening, and where God is at work among us will help preachers view the holy day and, if used, the prescribed texts in ways that will invite the listeners into mourning and dancing as together we remember God's saving work in Jesus Christ.

The Longest Night

I write this in the middle of the season of Advent . . . in the middle of a seemingly endless pandemic . . . in the middle of a massive recovery effort following one of the most devastating tornadoes in US history . . . in the middle of economic fears and ongoing political turmoil. And those are just a few of the corporate issues bringing darkness upon us. They are compounded by personal struggles and loss. The "earworm" that is playing in my head this season is my own Advent version of a popular Christmas song: "We need a little Advent, right this very minute!" Yes, we need some Advent hope. Each year, different tragedies seem to bring ever-deepening darkness upon us as the days grow shorter and the nights longer in the northern hemisphere. It's not that the rest of the year doesn't have its light-eclipsing moments. It does. But the despair that falls upon us at this time of year feels even darker in contrast to the "most wonderful time of the year" Christmas portrayed all around us.

What is going on? While it is not yet a specific day on the liturgical calendar, more and more churches are holding "Longest Night" or "Blue Christmas" services sometime during Advent, often to coincide with the longest meteorological night of December 20 or 21. What is going on in these special services is an acknowledgment that while Advent is a season of hope and joy as we anticipate the coming of Christ, hope and joy are easily eclipsed for many by the darkness of despair caused by personal and corporate pain. Creating sacred space where that pain can be named and turned over to God, then, is an act of pastoral care. The purpose of a Longest Night service is similar to that of a service of healing and wholeness but in the context of Advent's message that Light is coming into our darkness.[6]

Who is listening? When we lead a Longest Night service, the listeners may well be a combination of church members and guests. If the service is advertised to the community, it will surely draw people from beyond one's own congregation—perhaps even people who have little or no faith commitment but are in need of solace amid personal pain such as grief and loss. All who come to the service will be seeking some shred of hope to grasp when everything around them seems to be unraveling. With the support of Scripture, prayer, poetry, music, and candlelight, a preacher can offer words that usher the listeners into a quiet, holy place in the presence of God, where a glimmer of light might shine in their darkness. But providing such a space not only brings people into the healing presence of God; it brings them into the healing presence of the community. During Advent 2021, the world learned of the death of author and activist bell hooks. Several articles recounting her life quoted words from her book *All about Love*, including these: "Rarely, if ever, are any of us healed in isolation. Healing is an act of communion."[7] Those words are the perfect description of the healing power inherent in the community that gathers for a service on the Longest Night.

Where is God? We feel the presence of God in the gathered community—the community that remembers that, because of the birth of Christ, "the light shines in the darkness, and the darkness did not overcome it" (John 1:5). Nor will that darkness overcome us. But just as we are assured that hope will break through our darkness, as the sun will break through after the longest night, we are also assured that God accepts our sadness and stands with us as the Word who "became flesh and lived among us" (John 1:14). A number of other Scripture texts point to the ways in which God is present in our pain:

Psalm 103:8 "The Lord is merciful and gracious."

Isaiah 9:2 "The people who walked in darkness have seen a great light."

Isaiah 40:1 "Comfort, O comfort my people."

Matthew 11:28 "Come to me, all you that are weary."

John 14:1 "Do not let your hearts be troubled."

John 20:24–29 "Do not doubt but believe" (for the Feast of Saint Thomas on December 21).

1 John 1:5 "God is light, and in [God] there is no darkness at all."

Revelation 21:4 "Mourning and crying and pain will be no more."

The Longest Night service welcomes our sadness—our mourning and crying and pain—and invites us to melt our personal pain into that of the Christmas story, where we see the pain that gave birth to the incarnation. But out of that pain came the hope for all the world. Our celebrations of Advent and even Christmas do not end the night, but they *do* promise us hope for the dawn. In the presence of God and one another, we find a place to share our lament and mourn our losses, but together we hold on through the longest night: "Till thy mercy's beams I see; till they inward light impart, cheer my eyes and warm my heart."[8]

Christmas and Easter

While working on this chapter, I had a conversation with an Episcopal priest who had just presided over the funeral of a close family member. We talked about the challenges of preaching on special occasions like weddings and funerals. I shared with him the work Donna and I were doing on our book about preaching on such occasions. He then admitted that while he found preaching at funerals and even weddings challenging, the days on which he most dreaded preaching were Christmas and Easter!

Most laypeople would probably find it hard to believe that preachers fear preaching on the two holiest days on the Christian calendar, and yet most ministers would understand that priest's sentiments. Certainly there is a unique joy in gathering with God's people on the days that most clearly define our faith, but that joy is easily tempered by questions: What *really* has brought these people to church this day? Who might be listening? What do they expect to hear? Is there anything left to say that hasn't been said before? And how are these ancient stories relevant to modern lives?

Volumes have been written over the centuries about the Christmas and Easter texts—and even about how to preach them. It feels rather futile to try to add anything new in these few paragraphs. But here, I offer preachers some ideas to at least think about as they approach the Christmas and Easter texts.

What is going on? When we celebrate these high holy days, we are reaffirming the central beliefs of our faith: God's saving work on our behalf in the incarnation and resurrection of Jesus Christ. That seems clear enough. But debates about how we interpret and respond to them have fragmented the Christian community since the days of the New Testament church. Preachers will need to decide how much of their personal interpretations of the events of Christmas and Easter they are willing to share while also inviting the listeners to find their own meaning in the stories.

Who is listening? The unusual mix of listeners gathered for worship on Christmas Eve or Day and Easter Sunday is one of the reasons preachers dread preaching on those days so much. We all have had the experience of standing in front of a packed church on Christmas Eve or Easter Sunday, wondering if we somehow wound up in the wrong church! "Who *are* these people?" we ask as we see visitors, family members, and rare attendees looking back at us. It is easy to become jaded about those who have gathered and to wonder whether they are present by choice or obligation. The preacher's responsibility is not to judge but to invite our listeners to hear again the old, old stories and to point to ways we see them becoming new in our lives and world.

———

Where is God? The texts for Christmas and Easter, whether we find them by way of a lectionary or preacher's choice, have one thing in common: they ask us to believe some pretty amazing things—amazing things about God, the people God uses, and ourselves. The Gospel accounts of Easter (and, we might add, Christmas) are full of what Rowan Williams, former archbishop of Canterbury, calls "painfully untidy stories." They are "irregular and unconventional," Williams adds, "because whatever lay behind them was unexpected and deeply bewildering."[9] That is a helpful way to begin trying to answer the question "Where is God?" in these special days. The stories show us that God is with the people and in the places we least expect and might even question. God is in the vulnerable child and with the confused parents and poor shepherds and humbled kings of the Christmas story. God is with the terrified women and skeptical disciples of the Easter story. And because of that, God is with the vulnerable, the confused, the poor, the terrified, the skeptical, and the wounded today. In other words, God is with *us*.

No matter where we are on our journeys of life and faith, we all need to know the presence of the One who came and "pitched a tent" (John 1:14) among us, promising never to leave or forsake us—the One who rose to new life so that we, too, can have hope for resurrection in what feel like moments of death in our lives and relationships and world. The greatest gift we can give our listeners on Christmas and Easter is an invitation into the mystery and wonder of God's work in Jesus Christ, work that continues if we but open our eyes to see it. We can invite them to look for "the beautiful fallout of the resurrection in all of life."[10] We can point to examples of love conquering hate, hope healing despair, and new life springing forth from what appeared to be dead. And so, at Christmas and Easter, preachers have the high, holy privilege on these high, holy days of inviting our listeners to dance with all of God's creation, celebrating the incarnation and resurrection of Christ as we follow him into the world.

Christ the King / Reign of Christ

The liturgical year that begins on the first Sunday of Advent with apocalyptic texts about the dramatic and unexpected coming of the Son of Man ends in a similar way with Christ coming into his glory to rule over all things, reminding us of the cyclical nature of our life in Christ. We celebrate the reign of the One who was, and is, and is to come, inviting us to have a keen awareness that while we have not yet witnessed the arrival of God's promised kingdom—a promise that is renewed in Advent—that kingdom is already blossoming among us and calling us to work for God's justice and peace. We are reminded that "in Christ all things began, and in Christ all things will be fulfilled."[11]

The acknowledgment of Christ the King Sunday is often eclipsed by the secular celebration of Thanksgiving at the end of November. Further, the disregard for this holy day is reinforced by our modern sensitivity to patriarchal and imperialistic imagery, which has made its celebration problematic for many. Renaming and reshaping the day as Reign (or Realm) of Christ Sunday has tempered much of the concern about the image it portrays, but it remains an often overlooked day. Recapturing the significance of the day, however, can offer both hope and comfort as we are reminded of God's rule over all things.

What is going on? That reminder of God's gracious rule is what is going on as we celebrate the reign of Christ. Such a reminder is especially important when life seems to be spinning out of control—and it was just such a moment in the history of the world that gave birth to this special day. The "Feast of Christ the King" was decreed in a papal encyclical issued by Pope Pius XI in 1925, a time of great turmoil in the world. Pius XI recognized that he served the church in chaotic times and declared that the Lordship of Christ was the only hope for the world. So he established the Feast of Christ the King as, he stated, a way of combatting "the manifold evils in the world."[12] Understanding the origin of this holy day opens up an abundance of preaching possibilities as preachers and people consider how Christ's eternal rule shapes our lives.

Who is listening? The listeners on the Reign of Christ Sunday will probably include faithful church members along with some Thanksgiving-minded guests, depending on when these occasions fall in a given year. At the end of November, listeners will surely come to church with a mix of anxiety and anticipation as the holiday season shifts into high gear. Taking time to mark this transition Sunday between ordinary time and the season of Advent offers our listeners a moment to step back and look at the big picture of what our Christian faith means and the obligations it entails.

———

Where is God? The lectionary texts for the day provide a clear answer to the question asking where we see God on this occasion. God is the Shepherd who leads us "beside still waters" and "restores" our souls (Ps 23:2–3, Year A), the True Shepherd who will "seek the lost" and "bring back the strayed," "bind up the injured" and "strengthen the weak" (Ezek 34:16, Year A). God is the One who "raised [Jesus] from the dead and seated him at his right hand in the heavenly places" and "put all things under his feet" (Eph 1:20, 22, Year A).

Preachers will want to note the paradoxes evident in the texts for this Sunday. The Shepherd is the One who cares tenderly for the sheep but also the One who judges "between sheep and sheep, between rams and goats" (Ezek 34:17, Year A). The Son of Man invites into the kingdom those who have shown kindness and generosity in response to the blessings they have received from God's goodness but condemns those who have failed to share those blessings (Matt 25:31–46, Year A). God made Jesus Christ "the ruler of the kings of the earth" (Rev 1:5, Year B) and the One who has "come to have first place in everything" (Col 1:18, Year C), but he came into the world as an infant born of lowly circumstances and was mocked as "King of the Jews" as he hung helpless on the cross (Luke 23:37, Year C).

Another important theological theme that points to the ways of God on this Sunday is that of inheritance. Like most inheritances, this one is not earned but given to us out of God's abundant goodness. There is no *quid pro quo* here, no bargaining that promises God will bless us with the "riches of his glorious inheritance" (Eph 1:18) if we do certain things in return. No, the blessing God bestows upon us in the eternal reign of Christ is a gift of grace. And in response to that great gift, we offer our gratitude and our service, a logical connection to the season of Thanksgiving for preachers seeking to address the two occasions. We demonstrate our gratitude to God by feeding the hungry, clothing the naked, and caring for all God's sheep. Through his resurrection and reign, Jesus Christ "frees us to do more with our lives than protect them," as Lutheran theologian Walter Bouman declared. "We are free to offer them. We are called to love the world, to want clean air and water for everyone, to give ourselves to the service of peace . . . to commit to the cause of justice. . . . That is a big order. But you are free to pursue it by the resurrection of Christ, who has put an end to the dominion of death. We are free for the battle because the victory is already won."[13]

"[God] has put all things under [Christ's] feet" (Eph 1:22). "We are free for the battle because the victory is already won." Both statements are reminders that the Reign of Christ Sunday is truly a day for dancing. It is a day when we "rejoice, give thanks, and sing," as one appropriate hymn says, in response to God's triumphant work in Christ, assured that no matter the chaos that swirls around us or dwells within us, in the words of medieval mystic Julian of Norwich, "all shall be well; and all manner of thing shall be well."[14]

Holidays

While holy days strengthen our relationship to God, holidays strengthen our relationships with one another. They also remind us that we are citizens of a temporal nation and world as well as citizens of the kingdom of God and that God rules over *all* our commitments and allegiances. Holidays are opportunities for the church to engage with culture, as theologian James Calvin Davis suggests, "in the hope that its presence in the culture will help transform the human community in ways that more closely resemble God's intentions."[15] Our national celebrations "provide us an opportunity to level Christian theology as a critical lens on values and norms in popular culture" while, at the same time, they "lend a critical lens to the ways we American Christians practice our faith, calling us to deeper degrees of faithfulness."[16] The holidays below provide examples of how we can think about preaching on national holidays by asking what is going on, who is listening, and where God is present and at work. These and all our national celebrations invite us to both mourn and dance as the faithful people of God.

Martin Luther King Jr. (MLK) Day

The national holiday that celebrates the life and legacy of Dr. Martin Luther King Jr. occurs on the third Monday in January, making the day before that celebration the perfect time to acknowledge it in worship. For a number of years, preachers have taken the opportunity to mention the day in sermons, perhaps using an example from the life of Dr. King or quoting one of his writings in the sermon. In light of the awakening of our national consciousness over the past few years to lingering issues of racial injustice, the proclamation of the ways God calls us to live into a vision of peace and justice for all as exemplified by Dr. King has become more urgent.

———

What is going on? Like many national celebrations, MLK Day, as it has come to be called, has a vastly different meaning depending on one's perspective—in this case, one's racial/ethnic identity and socioeconomic location. What is going on is not only the recognition of the accomplishments of one man but also the realization of how much more we are required to build on those accomplishments to establish the "beloved community" of his dreams. Some will regard the day as a time for dancing in celebration of the racial barriers that have been broken down in our nation over the past several decades. Others will regard it as a time for mourning the racial evils embedded in our national history and the ways they persist even today. For all of us, the day should evoke both mourning, resulting from an honest acknowledgment of past and present realities, and dancing as we join hands and hearts in commitment to a better future.

———

Who is listening? Given the fraught nature of the MLK holiday, serious thought about our listeners is extremely important. Who we expect to be seated before us will shape our proclamation on this important day. If we choose to acknowledge the day in Sunday morning worship, we probably will find ourselves looking out upon our usual congregations. Those of us who serve predominantly white congregations may encounter an eagerness to learn and find ways to hold our nation accountable to its proclamation of justice for all. We may also face some degree of resistance. Those who serve congregations of color may encounter an eagerness for celebration and thanksgiving but also justified feelings of anger and despair. All of those listeners with their emotions will surely be present among those gathered for community ecumenical or interfaith celebrations of the day.

—————

Where is God? What, then, is a preacher to say? Perhaps a place to begin is with the acknowledgment that we all come to the MLK holiday with different perspectives depending on our identities and life experiences. With that reality in mind, we can begin to seek common ground in our Christian commitments: commitments to the beliefs that we are all created in the image of God and equal in God's sight, that God wills peace and justice for the human community, that we are all tainted by sin but also redeemed by the grace of God in Jesus Christ, and that God empowers us to press on in our work for justice even if it remains incomplete. These are some of the places where we can discern the presence of God on a day that evokes mixed emotions.

Appropriate theological themes along with texts can be found in the lectionary readings for the day before the MLK holiday. The Revised Common Lectionary offers a text (or two or three) for each lectionary year that can be viewed through a lens of the life and work of Dr. King, such as the following:

> **Isaiah 49:1–7 (Year A)** God chooses us even before birth and strengthens us as we fulfill that call.
>
> **1 Corinthians 1:1–9 (Year A)** Paul reminds us that God is faithful to those who have shown faithfulness and will strengthen us "to the end."

131

John 1:29–42 (Year A); **1:43–51 (Year B)**	Jesus calls disciples and invites them to "come and see" the work he is doing.
1 Samuel 3:1–20 (Year B)	God calls the boy Samuel to be a prophet of the Lord.
Psalm 139 (Year B)	God knows us and is with us always, even in times of darkness.
Psalm 36 (Year C)	We resist evil as we trust in God's love and protection.
1 Corinthians 12:1–11 **(Year C)**	A variety of spiritual gifts are given to us to be used for the good of the community.

In addition to the lectionary texts for the day before the holiday, theological themes and texts for preaching can be found in the sermons and writings of King himself and in the many books and articles of the past few years that have helped us see more clearly and work more diligently on lingering issues of racial injustice.[17]

Calling communities of faith to carry on that work may be the most important focus of pulpit proclamation as we celebrate MLK Day. Many congregations and communities commit to a day of service to honor King. Tragic events involving race over the past few years have made those of us who seek to live into King's—and God's—vision of the "beloved community" realize how far we have fallen short of that goal. The MLK holiday enables us to connect King's vision with the vision of the kingdom of God Jesus called us to pursue. One sermon is barely a step in the journey toward fulfillment of that vision, but it is a start. And coupled with honest conversation and community engagement, we can move toward the day when "justice roll[s] down like waters, and righteousness like an ever-flowing stream" (Amos 5:24).[18]

Days Celebrating Family/Human Relationships
Perhaps the best advice I ever received about preaching on days such as Mother's Day and Father's Day came from my graduate school mentor. When a colleague asked him how we should address those days in sermons, he responded, "Don't even think about it!" That might have been a reasonable approach for someone who preached only as a guest, but it is not as easy as that for those of us who serve congregations. Many church members have a deep emotional investment in the days that honor parents, demonstrated by the fact that church attendance on Mother's Day is often only eclipsed by attendance on Christmas Eve and Easter. Increasingly, however, it has become what Ellsworth Kalas calls "a perilous day" for preachers, given the fact that in recent decades, our society has become more transparent in acknowledging the pain and complexities surrounding the concepts of motherhood and, indeed, of all familial relationships.[19]

What is going on, and who is listening? Mother's Day, interestingly enough, has religious roots, having been celebrated in several congregations before being declared a national holiday in 1914. More than a century later, in response to a broadening understanding of the importance of other family relationships, days such as Father's Day, Grandparents' Day, and Adoption Day have been added to the calendar. What is going on when we acknowledge such days is a need to recognize, honor, and even celebrate the family ties that bind us to one another. That's a noble gesture, but it is complicated by our contemporary awareness of both critiques of our traditional understanding and new expressions of "family." Many people have come to define "family" by means of emotional ties rather than bloodlines. Modern lifestyles have rendered single-parent—either mother or father—families commonplace, and the LGBTQ+ community has broadened our understanding of families. What were once labeled "nontraditional families" are now part of the fabric of our congregations and communities. Members of both traditional and nontraditional families who are part of the church as well as their own family members and other visitors will be among the listeners on days celebrating family relationships. Sensitivity to the variety of listeners present will be important in shaping the sermon.

In addition to the complex definition of "family," preachers seeking to address any kind of family celebration must be mindful of the vast array of emotions carried by many of those who are listening. While some listeners will be eager to celebrate and give thanks for the families that shaped them, others will be rendered sad or even angry as they recall loss or abuse or regret.

————

Where is God? Given the challenges posed by speaking about families in any context these days, one might be tempted to acknowledge the day only briefly in a prayer or the announcements. But asking where and how God is present in our closest human relationships might just serve to turn mourning into dancing as we look honestly at those relationships in the light of Scripture and the abundant grace of God. The Bible is replete with stories about and references to families, but few of them are portraits of what we would call "happy families." And many of those references have been used to justify the subjugation or even abuse of family members, especially women and children. However, some biblical images of families help us see what God intended family relationships to be:

- the mother and sister of the infant Moses, who conspire to save him (Exod 2:1–10)
- Ruth, who refused to abandon Naomi (Ruth 1)
- King David, who cries out in despair over the death of his son Absalom (2 Sam 18:33)
- Jesus, who laments the faithlessness of Jerusalem as a mother hen who seeks to gather her brood (Matt 23:37)
- God, a loving parent who nevertheless is willing to give God's only Son for our redemption (John 3:16)
- Mary, who keeps vigil at the foot of the cross and whom Jesus entrusts to "the disciple whom he loved" (John 19:25–27)
- Paul, who mentors Timothy, "my loyal child in the faith" (1 Tim 1:2)
- Christian believers, who are addressed frequently in New Testament epistles as "brothers and sisters," "children," "the family of faith" (Gal 6:10), or "the family of believers" (1 Pet 2:17)

And we continue to see the work of God among us, bringing people into relationship with one another: in the creation of new life that gives rise to generation after generation; in the joining of individuals in the covenant of marriage; in extended family members, friends, neighbors, and teachers taking responsibility for raising children; in the congregations that take seriously their vows to be "family" to one another as the baptized people of God; and in the love exhibited by communities that care for one another. Whether we are in families by bloodlines, choice, or accident, our relationships reflect God's intentions for creation. In response, we are called to honor and give thanks for those whom God has given us to love and to be loved by, even as we seek God's strength to move beyond or repair broken relationships.

Occasions that celebrate family relationships are, indeed, "perilous" days to preach, but facing that challenge can help the listeners dance with thanksgiving for the ways in which their family relationships have reflected the grace of God while also mourning relationships that have failed to live up to God's intentions. Family days remind us that "faith, hope and love abide, these three; and the greatest of these is love" (1 Cor 13:13).

Patriotic Days

In October 2021, the Barna Research Group conducted a survey of more than five hundred clergy from a variety of Protestant denominations concerning job satisfaction.[20] The survey revealed that 38 percent of that group had left or considered leaving ministry during the previous year. The "straw that broke the camel's back" was the strain of trying to carry out effective ministry amid a ceaseless pandemic. But the "camel's back" had become weakened, most of them admitted, by increasingly polarized churches that reflect the deepening divisions in our society. The survey reminded me of a conversation I had recently with a former student, who lamented that no matter what he said from the pulpit, someone would take offense. He was desperately trying to faithfully seek a word from the Lord that would be heard and appropriated by all his listeners. But he learned that whatever word he conveyed would be met with criticism by some.

My former student's dilemma is far from unique. The question of what to say from the pulpit is on the mind of every preacher who is concerned about being true to the gospel, sensitive to the listeners, and faithful to one's own convictions. We can recall, however, that the Old Testament prophets faced such moments when calling the Hebrew people back to faith, Jesus faced such moments when deriding hypocrisy and injustice, and leaders of the early church faced such moments when challenging their followers to choose between divided loyalties. In American history, preachers have repeatedly faced divided congregations and fraught political times, most notably during the Civil War. Today, most preachers are preaching in what Lutheran pastor and professor Leah Schade calls "the purple zone," churches that reflect the so-called red-blue political divide.[21] And while we are hardly the first generation of preachers to seek to minister to divided congregations, the divisions are deeper and more pronounced due to technological, socioeconomic, and cultural factors.

What is going on, and who is listening? The divisions among us will surely be magnified on patriotic holidays. Like days celebrating family relationships, holidays such as Memorial Day, the Fourth of July, Labor Day, and Veterans Day are "perilous" days for preachers and best avoided or only briefly acknowledged in Sunday worship. But the reality is that many congregations—or a vocal cadre of members within them—have strong feelings about the connection between our national citizenship and our citizenship in the kingdom of God. The question of what is going on, then, will vary greatly depending on the stance of the listener, making the question of who is listening loom even larger in our preparation for preaching than on many other occasions. Most pastors will know where their congregation resides on the red-blue political spectrum and be sensitive to not only *what* to say but *how* to say it. Some listeners will be seeking a biblical and theological affirmation of their belief that God ordained America's role in the world as a "light to the nations." Others may be seeking forgiveness for corporate sins of the past or commitment to reshape the future. Some will be eager to name and celebrate the freedoms and blessings we enjoy; others will mourn the ways in which we have failed to share those freedoms and blessings. Some will want to honor those who fought and perhaps died in service to their country; others will want to see patriotic days as opportunities to "turn swords into plowshares" and "study war no more."

Where is God? Those deeply divided sentiments can lead us down some thorny paths when we ask where God is present on these patriotic days. Different listeners will have markedly different understandings of where and how God has been—and continues to be—at work in our national life. They will bring different understandings of what it means to be "one nation under God" and how we live into that identity. Even the use of Scripture on these occasions can be problematic, since so many texts have been invoked throughout American history to justify our exceptionalism or defend our mistakes. Perhaps most needed on patriotic days are sermons that call us to thanksgiving, humility, and responsibility before God, as exemplified by Moses's speech to the nation of Israel in Deuteronomy 10:12–22. In that text, the people are called to love God and walk in God's ways by loving and caring for one another, coupling any sense of being chosen with the responsibility to pursue justice and demonstrate care for all. Preachers can point to places where people across human divides are working together to live into God's expectations of us as a nation: soup kitchens and food banks; refugee resettlement programs; and organizations that work for racial and economic justice, peace, and protection of the environment.

One possible guide for our proclamation on perilous patriotic days comes from an unlikely source: the patriotic hymn by Katherine Lee Bates, "O Beautiful for Spacious Skies." Beyond its sentimental images lie some profound theological themes that can shape our common thoughts and prayers as we acknowledge our national as well as Christian identities. It calls us to thanksgiving for the "majesties" of this land, the "heroes" who have fought and even died for the nation, and the "patriot dream" that brought our nation into being. But it also recognizes the "flaws" that have marred our corporate pursuit of that dream and petitions God to "mend" them and "refine" the treasure with which we have been blessed. Finally, it seeks God's "grace" as we move into the future, calling us to "servanthood," marking our successes according to their "nobleness" and regarding our gains as expressions of the divine.

Patriotic days are, indeed, a time to dance as we remember the abundant gifts that have been given to us as a nation and citizens within it. But patriotic days also call us to mourn the price paid for many of those gifts: the price in terms of human lives lost, opportunities denied, injustices perpetuated, and landscapes scarred. More than anything, such days challenge us to seek to do better as we move into the future with gratitude and recommit to living as "one nation under God."

———

Holy days and holidays allow us to engage in what Laurence Hull Stookey calls "anamnesis" and "prolepsis": remembrance of the past and anticipation of the future. They invite us to mourn in response to our losses and mistakes and dance in celebration of our accomplishments while seeking to live ever more faithfully in the present. "We keep these occasions," Stookey asserts, "in order that God may work in us through them and in our world through us."[22] Because God holds and blesses all our days, holidays and holy days assure us that, in the words of the Shaker hymn, "the dance goes on."

CHAPTER 8

Occasions beyond the Walls of the Church

Beverly Zink-Sawyer

A time to keep silence, and a time to speak.
—ECCLESIASTES 3:7

Early in my ministry, I received a telephone call several weeks before Christmas. The caller was the master of the local Masonic lodge. One of my parishioners, a member of the lodge, had suggested me to be the speaker at the group's annual Christmas celebration for the members and their wives. Because the members' wives were to be included in the event, the lodge leaders thought it would be nice to invite the new young, female pastor—still a novelty at the time—to do the service. The format would be a brief worship service with hymns and prayers and a "message," as it was described, with the event to be held in the sanctuary of the Masonic hall, a rare moment when non-Masons were invited into the space.

That request was the first of countless similar invitations to come over the course of my years in parish and academic ministries. Those invitations included a prayer breakfast before the installation of new county commissioners, a high school baccalaureate service, and a presbytery-wide women's retreat held at a state park. A poll of my clergy colleagues has revealed such varied preaching occasions as military installations, a German Day celebration, protest rallies, Earth Day observances, a blessing of the animals, a Memorial Day parade and ceremony, and Sunday worship for prison inmates. Some of these were requests for a clergyperson to preach for what was an obviously religious event. Others came as requests for the preacher to give a "talk," "bring a message," "say a few words," or simply "offer a blessing" for a secular celebration. Sometimes the gathering was a recognizable worship service. At other times, the event included only a hymn or prayer or Scripture reading. Sometimes the topic would be clear from the occasion itself or would be given to the preacher. At other times, the topic of the sermon would be left up to the preacher. And since the gatherings were rarely held on a Sunday or in a liturgical context, there were no appointed lectionary texts.

As any experienced preacher will confirm, preaching can occur in more ways and places than we can imagine. There is surely a gift of grace in that reality, since preachers are invited into hidden and holy spaces in people's lives as they experience special moments of our shared humanity. To speak a word from the Lord, often when the listeners are at their most vulnerable, is a unique and precious privilege. These "beyond the walls of the church" occasions carry not only the usual challenge to address the occasion in a meaningful way but also layers of complications related to the location of the event and, often, the diversity of the gathered listeners. That said, such preaching occasions can provide some of the most important opportunities for offering a word of comfort or challenge or thanksgiving to people who might not otherwise hear it. They are opportunities for evangelism in its truest sense: the sharing of the "good news" of the gospel.

When people gather in a church building for any liturgical event, most carry with them certain expectations. They expect the service to be worshipful and reflect the theological—even denominational—commitments of the pastor and congregation. They expect a certain pattern of worship, an *ordo*, to shape the occasion. They even expect the very worship space itself to enhance what is heard and experienced. Many special worship occasions, however, occur outside the walls of the church and sometimes in spaces that have no walls at all, creating challenges for the preacher and people alike. There is no church building to signal that our gathering is for the worship of God. The familiar symbols and furnishings that aid our worship—such as a pulpit, a font, a Communion table, a cross, hymnbooks, and instruments—may be missing, leaving the preacher to create sacred space out of little or nothing at all.

What are we to do, then, when that space, no matter how lavishly or simply adorned, is missing? Envisioning the space and perhaps even visiting it beforehand, if possible, can help the preacher think about ways to shape the space for worship. Transportable objects such as crosses and candles are clear visual reminders of Christian worship. There might be ways to hang symbol-adorned banners and paraments on existing furniture or portable poles. At the very least, the preacher can read the Scripture text(s) from a Bible that is visible to all as a symbol of the centrality of Scripture for our worship and our lives of faith.

The important thing is that we find ways to bring our listeners in unusual venues into a holy, special place that will enable them to hear and respond to a message from the Lord.

The listeners who attend "beyond the walls of the church" preaching occasions add another unique layer of complexity to these events. While the listeners are always an essential part of sermon preparation, as we have demonstrated, they become both more important when discerning an appropriate message and more difficult to identify as the occasions move farther and farther beyond the walls of the church into a variety of often secular spaces. While we have emphasized throughout this book that it is impossible to imagine all the listeners who might be gathered for a particular preaching occasion, we can make at least some assumptions about congregational gatherings for worship. Once we move outside the church to secular spaces and events, few of those assumptions remain valid. Most "beyond the walls of the church" occasions will be marked by a vast array of listeners who carry with them any number of beliefs, ideologies, experiences, and expectations, challenging us to give more critical, imaginative thought to our listeners than we are required to do for most preaching occasions.

The categories below gather together many of the occasions or kinds of occasions preachers might be invited to address. While far from an exhaustive list, those named represent occasions my clergy colleagues and I have encountered in our ministries. Each set of occasions will give rise to different answers to the questions that ask what is going on, who is listening, and where God is present and at work, enabling the preacher to discern and share an appropriate word from the Lord.

Community Organizations and Celebrations

Vestiges of an era when Christianity had a high public profile remain evident in many corners of secular community life. A chaplain, who may be of any faith, opens each session of Congress with prayer. Clergy are invited to offer meditations or at least some kind of blessing at inaugurations of elected officials. Many schools, even public schools, hold baccalaureate services prior to graduation ceremonies. Whether such events are intended to continue our nation's tradition of civil religion or reflect a true desire to imbue a secular event with sacred significance, ministers receive many and varied requests for prayers, preaching, and sometimes simply their presence at community events, leading parish ministers to realize that they serve not only as pastors of local congregations but as chaplains to the community as well. We quickly realize that we represent far more than our own churches or even denominational traditions. Instead, we represent the broad religious commitments and values of the community. And when we as Christian preachers are invited to speak at secular events, we accept the responsibility to make clear and helpful connections between the occasion and gospel truths.

What Is Going On?

When we are invited to preach for special events sponsored by local organizations or community leaders, the reason for the event is usually obvious from the invitation extended to the speaker. The Masonic service I was asked to lead was part of the lodge's annual Christmas celebration. About a year later, I led a Thanksgiving service for the local Rotary Club. Both of those services were intended to mark a particular holiday, providing at least a general direction for the sermon. Some community organizations hold an annual prayer breakfast, inviting a minister from the community to speak. Usually, the speaker is asked to address a stated theme for the event. At other times, the subject of the prayer breakfast is simply prayer and what it might mean for individuals and the community at large. Communities also gather to show support for particular causes, such as the environment, LGBTQ+ rights, and most notably over the past few years, racial justice.

Local clergy are often invited to address those gatherings because of their role as community leaders as well as the desire of the sponsoring organization to connect the cause to the ongoing work of God. Most such community events are planned far enough in advance to give the preacher time to discern what is going on—what has prompted the occasion—and then identify an appropriate theological theme and text, but some events arise from crisis situations and demand an immediate response, as addressed in chapter 10. All "beyond the walls of the church" preaching, however, requires the preacher to be nimble and imaginative—and, most importantly, prayerful and humble—in thinking about the occasion.

Who Is Listening?

While the occasion of preaching for community events is usually pretty clear, the question of who might be listening is far more nebulous. In fact, discerning who might be present for any given event can be all but impossible, creating a significant challenge for the preacher. There surely will be individuals who are church members in attendance, but they will most likely represent many different churches, denominations, and even faith traditions. There will probably be religious skeptics and even nonbelievers present as well as individuals who are hostile toward the church. The challenge for us as preachers is to remain true to our calling to proclaim the good news of Jesus Christ while remaining mindful of those who do not share our theological convictions. Somehow, the preacher must find common ground among the many interests that brought such a diverse group together at this time and place. Finding that common ground is key to offering a message that might speak to at least most of those gathered.

When preaching for a service sponsored by a fraternal organization, we can make some pretty safe assumptions about the listeners and what brings them together. There is already a common bond among the members due to their shared interest in and commitment to working for the community. The motto of Rotary International is "service above self." Other organizations have similar statements of purpose. That expressed purpose—whether local service, international aid, or simply community bonding—is an important clue to understanding those who might be gathered for a particular event. Despite the many kinds of diversity represented within a service organization, the common ground on which they stand is caring for the community or world around them.

Other community occasions that occur outside the church will gather a disparate group of people but, as with service organizations, for a common purpose. A number of communities have Earth Day celebrations. Some churches sponsor "blessing of the animals" services that are held in parks or town squares and are open to the community. Protests and demonstrations for or against particular social issues draw diverse crowds of people who are focused on a common goal. And community crises tend to bring together people whose paths would otherwise never cross. Upon first glance, the listeners before us at a community event may appear to have little in common with us or with one another, but the organization or occasion around which they gather is an important common bond and provides the preacher with an essential clue to understanding who is listening.

Where Is God?

Once we get a sense of who is listening, we can begin thinking about the ways in which God is present and at work at this time and among these people. As noted above, community celebrations and civic events are usually focused on a particular theme or special observance or, in the case of crises, an immediate need, giving rise to some clear theological connections. Even then, however, the theme of the occasion might be very broad, leaving the preacher to think more deeply about ways to connect the occasion to the listeners. When I was invited to lead worship for the Masonic lodge, I was told it was their annual Christmas celebration—a rather general topic. But I was also told that the wives of the members would be present. I took that as a helpful clue, deciding on a message about the essential and empowering roles of women in the Christmas story. Using texts from the Gospel of Luke, I spoke of Mary, Elizabeth, and Anna as faithful witnesses to the identity of the infant Jesus as the promised Messiah, inviting all to believe and bear witness to God's gift of Jesus Christ in our own places and ways. In a similar way, when invited to speak at a Rotary Club Thanksgiving service, I connected the theme of the event (Thanksgiving) with those who would be present (business and community leaders engaged in community service). I encouraged the listeners to practice "thanks-living": living with gratitude for the resources they enjoyed and continuing to persist and "not grow weary in doing what is right" as they "work for the good of all" (Gal 6:9–10).

Some community preaching occasions will have clear connections to nature, enabling the preacher to point to the work of
God in creation and our responsibility to carry on that work
as caretakers of the world and all who dwell therein. Services
for the blessing of animals have become quite popular in many
communities. A sermon within such a service can draw from the
creation story in Genesis, the psalms that lift up our connection
to animals, and even the references to animals in the Gospels.
Earth Day and other environmental celebrations will remind the
listeners that, in the words of Psalm 24:1, "the earth is the Lord's
and all that is in it." We are merely stewards and not owners
of creation—the creation described in Psalm 8—and thus are
required to tend what God has given us in order to preserve it
and pass it on to future generations.

Among the most important community celebrations are
occasions that call us to care for God's people. The reawakening
to lingering racial disparities in our country that has marked the
past few years has challenged preachers to address those issues
within their congregations and beyond. Preachers have been
enlisted to address rallies before mass protests as well as community gatherings for peace and justice. The reason for those
occasions is usually quite clear, and those gathered, we can safely
assume, will represent a vast cross section of members of the
community. The challenge for the preacher will be pointing to
where God is at work in the situation and how we can live into
that work. If a rally is meant to inspire the pursuit of justice,
many powerful prophetic texts from the Old Testament would
be appropriate (Isa 1:17; Amos 5:21–24; Micah 6:6–8). If the
gathering is a service for peace, we can point to the gift of peace
Jesus gave to the world (John 14:27), a true peace that has "broken down the dividing wall" that separates us from one another

(Eph 2:14). If the event is in pursuit of equality, we can remind the listeners that we are all stamped with the image of God, as stated in the creation story, so that whether we are rich or poor, we "have this in common: the Lord is the maker of [us] all" (Prov 22:2). Perhaps the most powerful reminder of our equality comes from Paul's letter to the Galatians, assuring us that no matter our race or gender or status in the eyes of the world, "all of [us] are one in Christ Jesus" (Gal 3:28).

The trickiest of community events to address may be those connected to patriotic celebrations. We addressed this issue in chapter 7 in regard to preaching for national holidays. The same cautions apply even more here, given that the gathered listeners will probably be even more diverse than those sitting before us in church. The challenge is to find some common ground among the listeners. Despite the polarization that continues to plague our nation, we can regard even those whose political views differ from ours as the created and redeemed children of God, making us all equal in God's sight, as confirmed in the texts mentioned above. We can point to the gifts we have been given—gifts to be shared in community—and the hopes and dreams we have for ourselves, those we love, and all God's children. We can inspire generous hearts that are willing to listen and learn from one another and seek the common good.

Ministers are also often invited to participate in graduation celebrations at local schools and colleges. Sometimes they are asked simply to offer a prayer or benediction at the end of a graduation ceremony. At other times, they are invited to be the preacher for a baccalaureate service preceding the graduation itself. The reason for the occasion—the celebration of academic achievements and the beginning of a new phase of life—is clear, but like other community events, the composition of the listeners is less so. Even a diverse group of listeners at graduation events, however, shares some characteristics. The graduates themselves gather with joy and thankfulness and hope, celebrating their accomplishments and anticipating all that the future will bring. Those who have gathered to celebrate with them—family, friends, mentors—will have supported the graduates in many ways and through many years and wish them every success as they enter the next phase of life. Since graduation ceremonies are primarily for the graduates, we need to speak to them and invite the others gathered to "overhear" the ways in which God is present on the occasion. We can assure them that just as God has shaped their lives to this point, so God will lead them into the future (Jer 29:11; Prov 3:5–6). We can invite them to offer thanksgiving for the people and opportunities that brought them to this day (Jas 1:17; 1 Cor 1:4–5). We can caution them at this inflection point in their lives about the choices they will be called upon to make concerning whom and what they will serve (Josh 24:15). And we can remind them that the key to true success lies not in money or power or personal achievement but in Jesus's statement of the greatest commandment, charging us to "love the Lord your God with all your heart, and with all your soul, and with all your mind, and with all your strength" and to "love your neighbor as yourself" (Mark 12:30–31). "There is no other commandment greater than these," Jesus concluded, and no better word that we could speak to graduates moving into the future.

Community Health and Correctional Centers

The administrators of a variety of community facilities, including hospitals, mental health and correctional centers, and shelters, will at times invite local clergy to lead a worship service or Bible study or speak for a special event. Like many older adult communities, some of those facilities will have full- or part-time chaplains, but outside ministers are brought in to provide a variety of voices and perspectives for the diversity of individuals served by the facility.

What Is Going On?

The reason for the occasion is usually clear from the invitation. Many hospitals provide brief daily services—sometimes morning or evening prayer—for their patients. Those services might include a face-to-face component with ambulatory patients gathered in a chapel, but almost all such services are broadcast virtually through the hospital's video system. Most prisons and jails allow local clergy to lead worship services or Bible studies in the facility, sometimes with the celebration of the Eucharist. In a similar way, shelters for the homeless or for victims of abuse often provide worship and study opportunities for their residents. Whatever the venue, the purpose of the gathering will be obvious: to provide spiritual sustenance for people who are journeying through difficult times in their lives.

Who Is Listening?

At first glance, hospital patients, prison inmates, and residents of women's and homeless shelters appear to have little in common. Those listening will be individuals who represent many and varied socioeconomic, age, racial/ethnic, religious, and ideological characteristics. They will have experienced little or much of life. They will be abled or disabled to varying degrees both physically and mentally. Upon closer examination, however, we can see they have more in common than we might think, as many of them face uncertainty in the days ahead. Thus, when we ask who is listening, the answer is people who are experiencing similar emotions—fears and regrets, anger and shame, hopes and dreams. By naming those emotions, the preacher can begin to discern theological themes that declare God's presence and speak a word of comfort, assuring the listeners that they have not been left to dwell in dark places alone.

Where Is God?

The feeling that God—and everyone else—has abandoned them is probably the most common fear among those who are seriously ill or imprisoned or sheltered. Acknowledging that fear is a good place for preachers to begin thinking about the presence of God in ways that will speak to these listeners. A number of Scripture texts—most notably Jesus's own cry from the cross, "My God, my God, why have you forsaken me?" (Mark 15:34)—express the feeling of abandonment. Pointing to the humanity of Jesus in that moment can invite the listeners to see God as the One who suffers *with* them and upholds them in their distress.

Along with the feeling of abandonment that unites the otherwise diverse populations in health, incarceration, and sheltering facilities is the feeling of *waiting*. They wait for illnesses to be diagnosed and surgeries to be completed, for verdicts to be rendered and sentences to be finished, for circumstances to change and uncertainties to be resolved. God is in the waiting, we can assure them. We can encourage them to say, like the psalmist, "I wait for the Lord, my soul waits, and in his word I hope" (Ps 130:5) and remind them that "those who wait for the Lord shall renew their strength" (Isa 40:31). The Old Testament offers hopeful stories about waiting. The Hebrew people waited to escape from Egypt, waited to enter the Promised Land, and waited to return to their beloved Jerusalem after years of exile. The prophets waited for the people to turn from their wicked ways and to heed the promises of God. In the New Testament, the leaders of the early church waited through seasons of discouragement and even persecution for Christ's promised future glory (Rom 8:23; Titus 2:13).

To remind those who wait in dire and uncertain circumstances that God is present with them in their waiting is to offer them hope and comfort. The danger is offering them a false, simplistic hope. There are not always easy answers to the difficult questions of life. Sometimes the answers are even painful, if not devastating. Some illnesses *are* fatal, some prison sentences *are* excessive, and some relationships *are* irretrievably broken. All the faith in the world cannot change some circumstances. They need to be endured—but not endured without God's spirit, who "helps us in our weakness" even when we do not know how to pray and who intercedes on our behalf "with sighs too deep for words" (Rom 8:26). The manifestation of God's unfailing presence also comes in the form of all who stand by those who suffer. Friends and family, caregivers and counselors—all those who seek to live into Jesus's vision of the righteous in Matthew 25 by visiting the sick and imprisoned and offering shelter to those in need—are tangible reminders of God's care.

Beyond the similarity of emotions among those who are hospitalized, imprisoned, or sheltered are important differences depending on the setting. Those who are ill need to see God as the One who "heals all [our] diseases" (Ps 103:3). Those who are imprisoned need to see God as the One who "forgives all [our] iniquity" (Ps 103:3) and is "a God of justice" who "waits to be gracious" and "will rise up to show mercy" to us (Isa 30:18).

Those who are sheltered because of abuse need to see God as the One who made us in God's own image and commands us to love ourselves, even as we seek right relationship with others (Mark 12:31). Those who find themselves homeless need to see God as the One who shelters us under God's wings (Ps 91:4). Whatever the circumstances of those who find themselves in places of darkness, we can speak a word of hope, saying, "Be strong, do not fear! Here is your God. . . . He will come and save you" (Isa 35:4). God will calm your fearful hearts and save you from despair.

External Church Gatherings

Preachers are often invited to preach or lead worship for church-related events that take place beyond the church building or campus. Such events may be retreats sponsored by your own church or a neighboring church or group of churches. They may be denominational or interdenominational gatherings held at a retreat or conference center. They may be scheduled meetings of a judicatory. They may be brief worship services during a congregational or ecumenical mission project. Such events are important to the life of congregations, since they offer opportunities for members to grow in faith and service. Some church members will freely admit that their most meaningful faith experiences have come by means of participation in retreats and conferences. Many of us can still remember the messages we heard while sitting on log benches in rustic chapels carved out of the woods or the stories of faith shared with us around campfires. We have had "mountaintop experiences," sometimes while actually sitting on a mountaintop. We can recall being energized for the work of the church at a denominational gathering. Something about those events—whether the uniqueness of the venues or the fellowship of those gathered—makes us especially attentive to hearing a new word from the Lord.

What Is Going On?

In many ways, these external church events are the easiest "beyond the walls of the church" occasions on which to preach. The reason for the occasion is usually obvious from the nature of the event. Many congregations and ecumenical organizations have active women's and men's groups that hold special gatherings throughout the year such as prayer breakfasts, mission programs, and annual meetings. The events are meant to educate the participants, deepen their commitment to their faith and to the church, and perhaps inspire the members to share their time, energy, and resources with special projects. Congregation-wide and youth retreats are meant to do all those things as well as strengthen the bonds among the participants. Denominational gatherings are occasions to celebrate a shared faith and the ongoing work of a particular Christian tradition. The reason for and focus of the preaching occasion is usually quite clear.

Who Is Listening?

The identities of the listeners who might be gathered on these occasions are also probably obvious. Most of the participants will be members of a particular congregation or represent a group of congregations. We can assume, then, that they will be familiar with the language of faith and with the practices of the church. We are truly "preaching to the choir," as the saying goes, on these occasions. The listeners have chosen to participate in the retreat or conference and will be eager for the fellowship and learning offered, making them receptive to what the preacher might share. If the event is a meeting of a church group or judicatory, we can assume that the listeners are people who are engaged in the work of the church and support its ministries. There may well be "seekers," individuals open to but not yet committed to faith, in attendance at retreats or conferences.

The listeners gathered for a church-related event probably share a faith commitment, but they might have other characteristics to which the preacher must be attentive, especially in regard to their ages. Often, those characteristics are clear from the event itself, such as a youth retreat or a men's prayer breakfast or a women's conference. Being aware of the age and life experience of a majority of our listeners may shape not only the sermon itself but the style of its presentation. Younger listeners have been raised to apprehend information in ways different from their older counterparts. Being outside a traditional worship space can lead the preacher to present the message and engage the listeners in creative ways.

Where Is God?

Like other preaching occasions outside the church, these church-related occasions often come with a stated theme or topic or even a specified biblical text, providing ideas for answering the question of where we see God. Sometimes, however, the preacher is given little direction for the sermon. Assuming a faith commitment is already present, the sermon can become a means for strengthening that commitment and exploring new ways to deepen and express our faith. Retreats are meant to provide moments of pause in otherwise busy lives for renewal and inspiration. Stories of Jesus's withdrawal from the demands of his ministry suggest helpful texts for preaching. The Gospels record many times when Jesus went off by himself to pray, demonstrating the importance of prayer and reflection in renewing our faith (Matt 14:23, 26:36; Mark 1:35; 6:46; Luke 6:12; John 17). Conferences are meant to increase knowledge that strengthens discipleship and perhaps to envision the future of the church. Many texts from the Epistles about the work of the early church address Christian discipleship and the nature and purpose of ministry. Judicatory meetings are meant to gather members around the common goals of a denomination (often expressed in denominational statements) and assess the ongoing work of the church. Other themes appropriate for external church events include the following:

- living as faithful disciples in an increasingly secular world
- giving thanks for ministries of the past and present
- imagining and realizing a future for God's work
- working to transform lives and communities

Whatever the particular event, church gatherings held outside a church building offer some of the most satisfying preaching experiences. The listeners tend to be enthusiastic about their faith and attentive to new possibilities for spiritual growth. They are concerned about their congregations and the future of the church. They want to engage with the wider community in order to live out their calls to discipleship. Preachers and people together can find inspiration to "[go] into all the world and proclaim the good news to the whole creation" (Mark 16:15).

The "times to speak" a word from the Lord come to us in many and various ways. We honor that word and the people God has placed before us when first we are *silent* and listen attentively for what those to whom we speak might need to hear and, most importantly, for what God might have to say. Perhaps that is why the Ecclesiastes preacher deliberately placed "a time to keep silence" before "a time to speak" in this couplet. Preaching occasions that occur beyond the walls of the church can be especially challenging given the possibility of mixed and unpredictable audiences, unusual spaces, and extraordinary events. For the preacher to assume a silent, prayerful, expectant stance before attempting to speak is to recognize that we are merely the witnesses to and not the creators of God's word. Occasions beyond the walls of the church sometimes even provide opportunities to invite our listeners into a literal space of quiet before we break the silence with speech. However we shape the occasion and no matter what we are led to preach, may we never forget to listen first to the "still small voice" of God that echoes through our hearts and minds and those of our listeners (1 Kgs 19:12 KJV).

CHAPTER 9

Weddings and Divorces

Donna Giver-Johnston

A time to love, and a time to hate.
—ECCLESIASTES 3:8

When a couple gets engaged, they desire to begin writing their story of married life together. Beginning with "once upon a time," as is typical in fairy tales, they are hopeful it will end with "and they lived happily ever after." Couples I talk with want to begin their married life in the church. In our first premarital counseling session, I explain that as a pastor, I have dual roles. I act on behalf of the state, witnessing their vows and signing the license to legalize their marriage, and I act on behalf of the church, leading a worship service in which I ask God's blessing upon them and preach a sermon with theological reflections on love based on passages of Scripture like Ecclesiastes 3: "For everything there is a season, and a time for every matter under heaven. . . . [There is] a time to love. . . . [God] has made everything suitable for its time" (vv. 1, 8, 11).

At first blush, pastors might think that since weddings are joyful occasions—with love in the air and in the text—the sermon will be easy to craft. After all, pastors stand with the couple in their fairy tale in the making—between "once upon a time" and "they lived happily ever after"—and tell the story of God's abiding love. As preachers, we proclaim a word about the love of God and the ultimate expression of love between two people joined in holy matrimony. But in this time of skepticism about the chances of a couple staying married; in this time of secularism, when most people do not read the Bible or attend church regularly; in this time of consumerism, when weddings are like a three-ring circus and pastors are not treated as the ringmaster—in this time, most pastors would much rather preach at a funeral than a wedding, where their words are essential, not extraneous.

Even now (perhaps especially now), however, we are called to stand up at weddings and preach a word that witnesses to the timeless truth of God's love and our call to love one another. The most popular Scripture read at weddings, sacred and secular alike, is from Paul's first letter to the Corinthians, chapter 13. In his ode to love, Paul begins, "If I speak in the tongues of mortals and of angels, but do not have love, I am a noisy gong or a clanging cymbal" (v. 1). Then he goes on to describe what love is: "Love is patient, love is kind . . . love bears all things, believes all things, hopes all things, endures all things. Love never ends" (vv. 4, 7–8). The preacher's sermon seeks to testify to the promises of this Scripture—that love has the power to unite this couple in plenty and in want, in joy and in sorrow, in sickness and in health, as long as they both shall live. Despite promises made, all marriages do not live happily ever after. Some are marked by hate and end in divorce. Still, we are called to witness to the nature of God's abiding grace and eternal love, which endure all things. But how?

In the spirit of Ecclesiastes, which affirms that "there is a time for every matter under heaven," I claim that before you preach "There is a time to love" at a wedding, there is a time to ask questions: first, "What is going on?"; second, "Who is listening?"; and third, "Where is God?" Seeking answers to these questions will help you bridge the gap between the possible pandemonium of weddings and the proclamation of a meaningful word that sounds less like a noisy gong and more like the tongues of angels.

What Is Going On?

This question can easily be answered in one word: love. But defining love is not so easy. Ancient Greek contains several words translated "love." *Eros* is the passionate love that involves a deep physical attraction for another person. *Pragma* refers to the love shared by partners who are in a long-term committed relationship that will stand the test of time. *Agape* includes a compassionate love for humanity in general, and in Christianity, it encompasses the unconditional love of God. Seeking to define and describe love has occupied poets, writers, and musicians for centuries and continues to do so. "A Red, Red Rose" is a poem composed by Scotland's national poet, Robert Burns, first published in 1794:

> O my Luve is like a red, red rose
> That's newly sprung in June;
> O my Luve is like the melody
> That's sweetly played in tune.[1]

Since then, many poems, songs, and books have been written about the essence of love and the expression of love in marriage.

Louis de Bernières (author of *Captain Corelli's Mandolin*) pronounces, "Love is a temporary madness. It erupts like volcanoes and then subsides. And when it subsides, you have to make a decision. You have to work out whether your roots have become so entwined that it is inconceivable that you should ever part."[2] Max Ehrmann (author of "Desiderata") advises, "Neither be cynical about love; for in the face of all aridity and disenchantment, it is as perennial as the grass."[3] Judith Wallerstein (author of *The Good Marriage: How and Why Love Lasts*) writes, "A good marriage, as I have come to understand, is transformative."[4] Gillian Flynn (author of *Gone Girl*) admits, "To me, marriage is the ultimate mystery."[5] So then, we must wonder, what is love: madness or perennial? And what is marriage: transformative or mystery? Love and marriage are difficult to define, in part because of varied personal experiences with them—good and bad. In essence, a wedding is a ceremony that ritualizes the union between the passion of love and the covenant of marriage.

But marriage was not always "a time for love." In his twelfth-century treatise *The Art of Courtly Love*, Andreas Capellanus avows, "Everybody knows that love can have no place between husband and wife."[6] Marriage was long considered to be a legal transaction, and weddings were purely secular affairs. The medieval church's debate about the theology of marriage continued through the thirteenth century, when a consensus emerged: marriage is sacramental, even if the exchange of vows is made in private. It was not until the sixteenth century that the church played a larger role in matrimony. In 1563, the Roman Catholic Council of Trent ruled that marriage was a sacrament, instituted by Christ; thus, sacramental marriage became part of canon law, requiring that weddings must be performed by a priest. But even before that, Protestant reformers of the sixteenth century understood the public character of marriage—that weddings were to be performed in the church by a pastor who blessed the couple and instructed the congregation about God's will for marriage.[7] Protestant Reformers like Martin Luther and John Calvin used not sacramental but covenantal language for marriage and required witnesses to be present at wedding ceremonies inside the church. Subsequently, the theological meaning of a marriage ceremony was marked by ecclesial rites, as developed by Luther in 1529 and Calvin in 1542.[8] In 1549, leader of the English Reformation Thomas Cranmer produced the first prayer book to include complete services for both ordinary and occasional services in the Anglican Church of England. In the *Book of Common Prayer*, the rite for the celebration and blessing of marriage begins with the words of Archbishop of Canterbury Cranmer, articulating the deeply religious significance of marriage:

> Dearly beloved friends,
> we are gathered together here in the sight of God,
> and in the face of this congregation,
> to join together this man and this woman in holy
> matrimony,
> which is an honorable estate,
> instituted of God in Paradise,
> in the time of man's innocence,
> signifying unto us the mystical union
> that is betwixt Christ and his Church.[9]

The *Book of Common Prayer* clearly defines matrimony not just as the state or ceremony of being married but as holy, "instituted of God," set apart from the ordinary, lifted above the profane, and consecrated as sacred. Marriage is no longer to be viewed as just an estate, defined by interest or ownership or control, but instead as a "mystical union" with Christ. Therefore, it is to be regarded as honorable—characterized by principles of dignity, credibility, and esteem, worthy of high respect.

Appreciating the history and theology of marriage is only the first step in understanding what is going on at a wedding. Next, it is important to attend to how marriage is defined and celebrated by your denomination. Borrowing from the *Book of Common Prayer*, other denominations—including Lutheran, Methodist, and Presbyterian—published their own worship books that include marriage rites. In the *Book of Common Worship*, used by Presbyterian Church (PCUSA) congregations, the "Statement on the Gift of Marriage" begins a wedding service with these words:

> We gather in the presence of God
> to give thanks for the gift of marriage,
> to witness the joining together of N. and N.,
> to surround them with our prayers,
> and to ask God's blessing upon them,
> so that they may be strengthened for their life together
> and nurtured in their love for God.[10]

From the beginning of the ceremony, these words make clear what is going on at a wedding: as with any worship service, it is a time to gather in the presence of God. This gathering can happen in many different places. As you prepare for a wedding, consider the physical setting. Will the wedding be in a church? Is the church one you know well, or are you a visiting pastor? If possible, visit the space before the wedding to familiarize yourself with the surroundings. Will the wedding be outside in a yard or inside a house? Once, I was asked to do a wedding in a treehouse, but because of the larger than expected number of guests, the couple opted for the steps in their backyard. In order to keep his two young boys occupied, the groom gave them each a camera. They stood on either side of me snapping pictures the whole time! Whether it is in a church or in a treehouse, inside the nave or outside in nature, as pastors, we call people into the presence of God, affirming Jesus's promise, "For where two or three are gathered in my name, I am there among them" (Matt 18:20).

People who have gathered will know they are in the presence of God by the liturgy that can transform any space to sacred. The pastor begins with calling people to worship with sentences of Scripture: "God is love, and those who abide in love, abide in God, and God abides in them" (1 John 4:16); or "O give thanks to the Lord, for he is good; for [God's] steadfast love endures forever" (Ps 106:1). As you craft the worship service and consider the liturgical and musical selections, keep in mind your local church's wedding policies. Be ready to answer the bride's question about whether the photographer can capture every moment—up close and personal. Be ready to answer the groom's question about whether the recessional song can be AC/DC's "You Shook Me All Night Long." Be ready to answer the mother of the bride's question about whether the liturgy can include an homage to the deceased grandparents. Go over the order of worship with the couple, and have them meet with the musician to select appropriate music for the service. Be ready to suggest classic hymns like "Joyful, Joyful, We Adore Thee" and "Now Thank We All Our God" or contemporary hymns like "The Prayer" and "Love Has Brought Us Here Together." All of these contextual matters may seem extraneous to preaching, but they are all integrally related to connecting the worship to the word, the music to the message, helping people hear the word of God in this time and this place.

According to the "Statement on the Gift of Marriage," a wedding is a gathering in the presence of God "to give thanks for the gift of marriage." Marriage evolved from a secular arrangement to a sacred institution, but still with romance being a secondary concern. In America, it was not until the middle of the nineteenth century that love came to be an expected part of marriage. Since then, the pendulum has swung in the opposite direction, with love as the driving force of a wedding and practical economic concerns and religious rituals taking the back seat. In the twentieth century, traditional understandings of marriage gave way to more contemporary questions about the reproductive purpose of marriage, birth control, and same-gender marriage. Based on how they have answered questions about marriage, Christian churches have approved certain policies and now enforce certain prohibitions. As you seek to understand the context of the wedding you are officiating, it is important to know your denomination's theological understanding of holy matrimony and their practices that honor and uphold marriage. As you prepare to preach at a wedding, it is also important to ask, "What is going on in this particular church?" Different churches think of weddings in different ways: a ceremony, a blessing, a rite, a worship service, a sacrament. Some churches maintain Christian marriage is a right only worthy people can earn; others understand marriage, like grace, as a free gift offered by God to all. Consider how marriage is defined and weddings are celebrated in a particular community and how it is an occasion to give thanks.

In 2015, I was the new pastor of Community Presbyterian Church and was charged with leading a discussion on marriage and weddings. The Supreme Court had just affirmed that the US

Constitution guarantees a right to same-sex marriage, making it legal in all fifty states. In addition, the PCUSA had voted to permit same-sex marriages in churches where the session and the pastor agreed. I started the discussion by saying to the session that this was a big issue, and we were going to take our time, read Scripture, discuss, pray, and eventually decide. A woman raised her hand and said, "I'm ready to vote now." I said again, "This is a big issue, and we are going to take our time, read Scripture, discuss, pray, and eventually decide." A man raised his hand and said, "I'm ready to vote now." I asked, "Are you all ready to vote?" They nodded. I asked for a motion, and those present voted unanimously to allow same-sex marriages at our church. I asked, "Can someone please help me understand what just happened here?" One elder said, "We have seen where the road of intolerance leads—to our former pastor, who was gay, dying by suicide—and we don't want to go down that road again." The session voted to host same-sex weddings, and shortly thereafter, I officiated at our first same-sex marriage ceremony.

The title of my sermon was "At Last." It was based on the Scripture passage, "Clothe yourselves with love, which binds everything together in perfect harmony" (Col 3:12–17). Using the metaphor of dressing, I reminded the couple that love is not just romantic but routine, something that is as simple as daily dressing, choosing what you will put on as an act of love. At the same time, love is radical—powerful enough to change the hearts and minds of people. In the sermon, I shared a word of truth that in a time to love and a time to hate, and every time in between, God makes everything suitable for its time. And this was a time to give thanks for the gift of marriage—this marriage. At last. As the apostle Paul promises, "Love bears all things, believes all things."

Who Is Listening?

After attending to what is going on, our process of writing a sermon for special occasions continues with attention to those who participate in and attend the wedding ceremony and listen to the sermon. In the beginning of the rite of marriage, the *Book of Common Worship* helps identify who is listening by describing a wedding as a time "to witness the joining together of N. and N."

First, of course, think about who is being joined together, identifying who N. and N. are beyond their names. Are they a young couple getting married for the first time? Or is this a second marriage after a bitter divorce? Is this a mixed-gender or same-gender marriage? Is this a same-religion or an interfaith marriage? Before the wedding, it is important that you take some time to get to know the couple. I begin premarital sessions by asking the couple to introduce each other to me. How they talk about their partner is the first clue to who they are and how they show love and respect for each other. These conversations give me some personal information to use in the sermon—with their permission, of course. Using personal examples helps ground the sermon in the here and now, demonstrating that love is not just a poetic verse, "How do I love thee, let me count the ways"; rather, love is enacted in ordinary expressions, in living out the ways "I love thee": as Megan cleans the bathroom and Alex takes out the trash; as Ryan puts his career on hold for Addy and she welcomes his child from his first marriage. There is "a time to love," and that time is one action, one day at a time. Premarital sessions provide you the opportunity not only to get to know the couple but also to help them reflect on their vows and give them the tools to help improve their chances of staying married. Discussing the commitment of marriage before the wedding prepares them to declare their intentions when asked, "Understanding God has created, ordered, and blessed the covenant of marriage, do you affirm your desire and intention to enter this covenant?" with a firm "I do."

Second, imagine who might be coming to this wedding, including people in the wedding party and the congregation. Likely, there will be married couples—some of whom are happily married and others not. There will be individuals who are divorced—some angry and bitter and others just glad to be free. The father and mother of the bride who are not amicably divorced may need to sit in separate pews to keep the peace. Some people who are widowed may be grieving the loss of their spouse. Some people sitting in the pews will be sentimental about love and others skeptical. Others will be physically present but checking their phones until they can move on to the reception. Still others will joyfully celebrate, imaging themselves in an episode on the Hallmark Channel. Some of the family members and other guests will support the marriage and others may not. Whoever they are, they are gathered to witness the couple's joining together in holy matrimony. People come to a wedding to be witnesses to the vows the couple makes. The pastor will first ask the family members, "Do you give your blessing to the couple?" to which they answer, "We do." Then the pastor will ask the whole congregation, "Will all of you witnessing these vows do everything in your power to uphold them in their marriage?" to which they answer, "We will." Promising to love each other for life is not easy but is made more possible with people who pledge to help them keep their vows.

The people in the pews are not just observers; they are participants in the wedding ceremony as witnesses to the vows. They can also participate in the crafting of the sermon. Spending time considering who makes up the congregation puts pastors in a better position to preach a relevant word that will speak to the listeners. Imagine what the listeners are thinking and how they are feeling. What are they wondering about love, marriage, the couple, themselves—and God? What do they bring with them to the occasion (maybe joy and gratitude or maybe regret and shame)? What do they need to take from it (maybe a reminder that love is possible and powerful or an assurance of God's love, even when we fail to keep our promises to love)? Asking yourself what word the listeners most need to hear about love will significantly increase your chance of preaching that word. Keeping in mind that people come to weddings with a vast array of experiences of love and marriage, be careful not to shame and instead to let grace abound. Remember that people will not likely remember what you say in your wedding sermon, but they will never forget how you made them feel.

As you consider what is going on, you will understand the occasion as wedding and worship. And as you think about who is listening, you will recognize a couple making a covenant and the congregation witnessing to it. But no matter how much reflection and preparation you do, weddings are always full of surprises. My mother-in-law used to say to me, "You should write a book on weddings." The truth is, any experienced pastor could write a book on weddings—not just a "how to" manual but a humorous account of all of the wedding stories they have accumulated over time. How could I forget the groom who told me that he vomited when he was nervous—and he was feeling nervous on his wedding day—and so I had to put a paper bag in the chancel? I remember the flower girl who refused to walk down the aisle and another one who dumped all her rose petals within her first step and then ran the rest of the way down the aisle to her mother. There was the best man who forgot his tux and the groom who forgot the rings, and so we had to wait over an hour until we could start the wedding. There was the unity candle that would not stay lit because of the air-conditioning blowing on it, and there was the bride who almost fainted because there was no air-conditioning. I was amazed by the couple who led the congregation in playing "Will the Circle Be Unbroken" with kazoos! And how could I ever forget the Covid-19 wedding of four people: the couple, the cameraman, and me? Over my years of officiating at numerous weddings, I have found that while the couples are not always sure what it means to vow to love "'til death do us part," they know what they want in a wedding ceremony: perfection. This is the one thing that I can almost guarantee them that they will not have. I try to reassure them, saying, "Be glad when something does not go as planned, because it will surely be the one story you tell over and over again through the years." As the apostle Paul promises, "Love hopes all things, love endures all things."

Where Is God?

After better understanding what is going on and who is listening, our process of writing a sermon for a wedding culminates with asking, "Where is God?" In the "Statement on the Gift of Marriage," the *Book of Common Worship* locates God right in the center of the wedding service, in which all those gathered are called "to surround them with our prayers and to ask God's blessing upon them, so that they may be strengthened for their life together and nurtured in their love for God."[11]

When I meet with a couple seeking to be married in our church, I ask them, "Why do you want to be married in a church?" In between "It's a beautiful space" and "My mom would be horrified if we went anywhere else," I listen for any expression that they want a religious ceremony. I explain that a justice of the peace can marry them in a simple civil ceremony at the courthouse. But as pastor of a church, in addition to witnessing their vows and declaring them married, I preach a sermon from Scripture, and with the congregation, I surround them with prayers and ask God's blessing upon them using prayers like this:

> Gracious God,
> you are always faithful in your love for us.
> Look mercifully upon N. and N.,
> who have come seeking your blessing.
> Let your Holy Spirit rest upon them
> so that with steadfast love
> they may honor the promises they make this day.[12]

In essence, that is what a wedding in the church is about—testifying to the promise of God's love to abide with all of us, but especially this couple who have come seeking God's blessing in marriage. From the very beginning of the service, the pastor can begin to articulate these theological themes of marriage, communicating clearly that this wedding weaves together this couple's story of love with God's story of love. In Scripture and song, in prayers and proclamations, we have an opportunity and an obligation to reveal God's abiding presence and eternal promise of love.

During one premarital counseling session in which a couple and I were going over the elements of the service, I shared two versions of the words that might be spoken when they exchanged rings. The bride liked the one that read, "I give you this ring as

a sign of our covenant." The groom, who was usually immediately agreeable, was quiet. I asked what he was thinking. He
paused for a moment and then admitted the problem: "I am
embarrassed to say that I don't know what *covenant* means."
This presented an opening for explaining the theological meaning of *covenant* as a promise—in this case, a promise that they
make to each other—to love as long as they both shall live.
But they are not the only ones making promises at this time. I
remind them that their family and friends, as witnesses to the
covenant they make, are promising to pray for God's continued blessings throughout their married life together, to help
them keep the promises they make this day.

Covenant, or promise, is a powerful theme of a wedding
and the abiding theme of marriage; therefore, it should be a central part of the sermon. Other theological themes to explore in
a wedding sermon include love, faith, hope, commitment, sacrifice, forgiveness, fidelity, grace, and peace. Theological themes
will hopefully manifest themselves in the word proclaimed and
also in prayers of blessing. Take note of the theological themes
revealed in this portion of a prayer from the *Book of Common
Worship*:

Give them the grace when they hurt each other
to recognize and confess their fault,
and to seek each other's forgiveness and yours.
Make their life together
a sign of Christ's love
to this sinful and broken world,
that unity may overcome estrangement,
forgiveness heal guilt,
and joy conquer despair.[13]

Knowing it will be difficult to confess their faults and seek forgiveness in their married life together, I pray this prayer after the
sermon and vows but before the final declaration of marriage. I
pray that with God's blessing of grace, the unity of their marriage will endure, and their life together will be a sign of Christ's
healing love in this broken world.

It is our hope and prayer that this will be so. And despite
all the times we know estrangement will overcome unity,
forgiveness will not heal guilt, and despair will conquer joy,
still we stand in the hope that by the power of love, they may
be strengthened for their life together and nurtured in their
love for God. One of the most meaningful services I have ever
done was a renewal of wedding vows. This was a second marriage for a couple who had been married for thirty-five years.
Royce and Barbara were old and gray, witty and wise, faithful
and grateful. Their clothes were simple, and they were easily
satisfied with my suggestions. They wanted the service to glorify God, from whom all blessings flow, giving thanks for the
blessing of having shared life's journey with the one they loved.
For a Scripture reading, they chose 1 Corinthians 13 and nodded knowingly when I read love "bears all things, believes all
things, hopes all things, endures all things" (13:7). They had
surely experienced most if not "all things." A few years later, I
conducted the funeral service for Royce. As I watch Barbara
mourn his death while worshipping each Sunday from the
same pew they shared throughout their life together, she bears
witness to the scriptural truth, "Love never ends" (1 Cor 13:8).

Still, we recognize that marriage is a complex institution—
joining together the public and the private sector, society and the
individual. For Christians, marriage is both secular and sacred,
regarded as both honorable and holy, which makes preaching

at weddings all the more difficult. In fact, Protestant Reformer Martin Luther wrote in *The Estate of Marriage* (1522), "How I dread preaching on the estate of marriage! . . . The lax authority of both the spiritual and the temporal swords has given rise to so many dreadful abuses and false situations, that I would much prefer neither to look into the matter, nor to hear of it. But timidity is no help in an emergency; I must proceed. I must try to instruct poor bewildered consciences and take up the matter boldly."[14] If you, like Luther, find yourself dreading preaching at weddings, one way to take up the matter boldly is to focus, like he and the other Reformers did, on Scripture.

But what Scripture text should be read for a wedding? In the Gospels, the only reference to Jesus at a wedding takes place not when he is preaching but when he is performing his first miracle, turning water into wine (John 2). The pastor might jokingly be called upon to perform such a miracle at the reception, but at the church service, we are expected to preach a sermon. Liturgical scholar Kimberly Bracken Long admits, "Anyone who has tried to choose Scripture readings for a wedding knows that the Bible does not say much about marriage—and that what it does say is not always helpful! Scripture offers an array of models for marriage, including polygamy and concubinage."[15] While Long admits, "Few biblical passages speak directly about marriage as the egalitarian and mutually minded relationship that many contemporary Christians assume," still she believes "Scripture is a living Word that continues to speak into every time and place."[16] In worship planning, I offer couples a choice of Scripture readings for their wedding, providing some options to choose from. The following is a list of Scripture passages to consider using for weddings:

Ruth 1:16–17	Ruth expresses deep and abiding love to Naomi: "Where you go, I will go."
1 Samuel 18:1–3	David and Jonathan make a covenant to love each other as their own soul.
Psalm 100	A reminder that God's steadfast love endures forever.
Psalm 105:1–6	A call to "Let the hearts of those who seek the Lord rejoice."
Psalm 116:1–2, 12–19	"I love the Lord. . . . I will pay my vows to the Lord."
Ecclesiastes 4:9–12	The wisdom that "two are better than one" means "a threefold cord is not quickly broken."
Song of Songs 2:10–13	In springtime, the voice calls to one's beloved to arise and come away.
Song of Songs 7:6–13	The author describes his beloved's body as reflected in nature and admits desire for her.
Song of Songs 8:6–7	The power of love is "strong as death, passion fierce as the grave," such that "many waters cannot quench love."
Matthew 5:13–16	Jesus exhorts his followers, "You are the light of the world . . . let your light shine."
Mark 12:28–34	Jesus sums up the law to love God and love your neighbor as yourself.
Luke 6:37–38	Jesus gives a glimpse of grace: "Forgive and you will be forgiven. . . . The measure you give will be the measure you get back."
John 2:1–11	Jesus performs his very first miracle at a wedding, turning water to wine.

John 14:26–27 Jesus gives the gift of the Holy Spirit and peace the world cannot give.

John 15:9–17 Jesus commands his disciples, "Love one another as I have loved you. . . . I am giving you these commands so that you may have love for one another."

John 21:15–17 Jesus asks Simon, "Do you love me?" When Simon says, "You know I love you," Jesus says, "Feed my sheep."

Romans 12:9–18 Paul calls the church in Rome to "let love be genuine; love one another with mutual affection."

1 Corinthians 13:1–13 An ode to love: "And now faith, hope, and love abide, these three; and the greatest of these is love."

Galatians 5:14, 22–26 A summary of the whole law, "You shall love your neighbor as yourself," and the fruit of the Spirit, "love, peace, patience, kindness, generosity, faithfulness, gentleness, and self-control."

Ephesians 3:14–21 A prayer to "know the love of Christ that surpasses knowledge."

Ephesians 5:25–33 An entreaty for husbands to "love [their] wives, just as Christ loved the church and gave himself up for her," declaring that a husband should "leave his father and mother and be joined to his wife, and the two will become one flesh."

Philippians 2:1–13 A plea to "be of the same mind, having the same love. . . . Look not to your own interests, but to the interests of others."

Colossians 3:12–17	An invitation to "clothe yourselves with love, which binds everything together in perfect harmony."
1 Peter 4:8–11	A summons: "Above all, maintain constant love for one another, for love covers a multitude of sins. Be hospitable to one another without complaining."
1 John 3:18–24	A call to "let us love, not in word or speech, but in truth and action."
1 John 4:7–16	An invocation: "Beloved, let us love one another, because love is from God. . . . God is love, and those who abide in love abide in God, and God abides in them."

In addition to Scripture passages, couples might choose a poetic verse to be read during the wedding service. Some examples I have had requests for are Kahlil Gibran, Rumi, and Shakespeare. Using a Scripture text to interpret a poetic verse would make for a beautiful and powerful sermon.

Once you have chosen a Scripture passage, then you can interpret it and, with the inspiration of the Holy Spirit, discern a word to preach to the people on this occasion. Given the hype of weddings and the marginal place of clergy, many ministers decide to skip preaching a sermon, because they realize that no one is really listening anyway. I disagree with this decision. I have always preached a sermon—albeit a shorter one than an ordinary Sunday sermon—because I believe that it is an occasion to preach the gospel of the radical and inclusive love of God to people who might not otherwise hear it. And I believe that through my words, or even in spite of my words, divine grace is bestowed on all present—on the married and single, the attentive and distracted, the sentimental and skeptical alike. I preach a wedding sermon addressed to the couple themselves, with the congregation listening in. I preach fully aware that the couple will likely not hear or remember anything I say, due to nerves and the excitement of the day. After the wedding, I send them a copy of the sermon along with their copy of the marriage license, for which I have received deep appreciation. One couple even shared that on their anniversary every year, they read the sermon to remember the day of their wedding.

Whatever Scripture text we use, we preachers proclaim a message witnessing to the truth that there is a time to love, and God has made everything suitable for its time. A sermon on Psalm 100 or Song of Songs 8 or 1 John 4 may seek to weave together the couple's story of passionate love with the story of God's relentless love, which is the source of love and promises to never end. A sermon on John 15 or Philippians 2 may describe the sacrificial love of Jesus Christ as a model for the self-giving love we are called to in all relationships and especially in marriage. A sermon on John 14 may inspire all to trust in the presence of the Holy Spirit to help us live more faithful lives than on our own. A sermon on 1 Corinthians 13 may substitute the names of the couple for wherever it says "love"—"Deb is patient. Joe is kind. . . . Jared is not envious or boastful or arrogant or rude. Katie does not insist on her own way. . . . Alicia is not irritable or resentful. Amy does not rejoice in wrongdoing, but rejoices in the truth." A sermon can preach that when love is embodied and active, chances are better that their love will bear all things, believe all things, hope all things, endure all things, and never end.

Despite the couple's best intentions, the congregation's best support, and the pastor's best sermon, sometimes "a time to love" turns to "a time to hate." The promise of love gets twisted.

Conflicts are not resolved. Marriages end in divorce. Most couples part in a burst of anger or slink silently into the dark night of remorse, but there are other possibilities for marking the end of a marriage. While such rituals do not celebrate a breakup or bless a divorce, they do provide a time for two people to respectfully release each other from marriage vows in a sacred place, where they can receive assurances of forgiveness from each other and from God.

The power of such rituals is that they carry burdens that are too heavy for us to carry without them. In *God Believes in Love*, former Episcopal bishop Gene Robinson describes the ritual of divorce he shared with his wife. Together with the priest, they stood in the church where they were married, prayed for the forgiveness of each other and God, and prayed for their daughters, pledging to raise them together. Then they gave their wedding rings back to each other as a symbol of releasing each other from the wedding vows that they no longer held each other to. And finally, they shared the body and blood of Christ in a service of Holy Communion. Robinson reflected on the ritual of divorce: "It felt exquisitely holy as it was excruciatingly painful. Somehow we had just managed to end our marriage in a loving way and not just slink away from God under cloak of night."[17] Not all couples could do this, but all couples need to be reminded that God's promises continue even after divorce. Healing will hopefully come in time through pastoral care that offers reminders that "for everything there is a season" and reassurances that God's love endures forever—and, in fact, it never ends.

Doctors say that prevention is the best medicine. The same can be said about marriage. As I previously suggested, before you officiate at a wedding, make sure you offer premarital counseling to help couples "unpack their baggage" and discern if and how they will honor the promises they make to love each other with patience and kindness their whole lives long. I tell couples that it is up to them to choose to keep their vows each and every day of married life. I do not try to predict marital success; however, I do pay close attention during premarital counseling and give them tools to communicate, navigate conflict, and offer forgiveness, before and after they are married.

One couple I was working with in premarital counseling was young and head over heels in love, or so it seemed at first. As we began our sessions together, I noticed that the man interrupted, dismissed, and degraded his fiancé. He was abrupt and abrasive, bordering on being verbally abusive. I wanted to call off the wedding, but that was not my decision to make. And so, instead, I tried another strategy. After each time the man put down the woman, I simply asked her, "Did you hear what he said?" and asked her to repeat what she heard him say. At first, she was not even aware of what he was saying or how he was saying it. She simply didn't see it. Until she did. And then she called off the wedding. The groom's family was furious and left the church. Five years later, the woman contacted me to say she had found the right person and they were happily married. She called to thank me for giving her the courage to get out of an unhealthy relationship that would have surely ended in divorce, or worse. Trusting that there is a time to love and a time to hate and a time to love again, she believed wholeheartedly that God has made everything suitable for its time.

After understanding what is going on at a wedding, identifying who is listening, and discerning where God is in the covenant of marriage, it is time to craft and preach a sermon that is faithful to the biblical text and fitting to the context. Here is a paragraph from a sermon I preached on 1 Corinthians 13 on the power of love—human and divine—which, like all of my wedding sermons, I addressed to the couple.

> Love is not always laughing together; at times, it is solving tricky problems together; at times, it is sitting in painful silence together. Still other times, it is crying together, when life is more than we can bear alone. I invite you to walk through life together, side by side, hand in hand, because whether you skip over high mountain tops, or trudge through low, dark valleys—and you will do both, my friends—love will endure. When the day comes that death parts the two of you, you will be assured of the unending love you have shared and comforted by the love of God. In the time you have together, I invite you to commit yourselves to the difficult but rewarding task of never letting your love end. For if you do, you will be blessed in having shared life's journey with the one you love.

Despite what anyone else might say about a pastor's marginal role in a wedding, you have an important part to play. As a pastor standing between a couple's story of "Once upon a time" and "They lived happily ever after," you witness their vows, surround them with your prayers, and preach a sermon that tells a story of covenantal love, which bears all things, believes all things, hopes all things, and endures all things. And you ask God's blessing for a love that never ends.

CHAPTER 10

Crises and Tragedies

Donna Giver-Johnston

A time to kill, and a time to heal.
A time for war, and a time for peace.
—Ecclesiastes 3:3, 8

I began writing this chapter on 9/11—a day when we remember the horrific events that occurred on September 11, 2001. On that infamous day, terrorists hijacked airplanes and flew them into the twin towers of the World Trade Center in New York City and into the Pentagon in Washington, DC. Another plane appeared to be headed toward a target in DC (likely the Capitol), but its mission was foiled by heroic passengers who stormed the cockpit, resulting in a deadly crash in Shanksville, Pennsylvania. These attacks on the United States killed 2,977 victims, injured countless others, and compromised the health of many thousands of first responders for years to come. It also traumatized all of us who watched it unfold before our eyes. Those of us who were old enough to understand what was happening remember where we were that day when we heard the devastating news that left us feeling shaken and vulnerable, wondering if this was the end of the world as we know it.

I remember I was living in New Jersey and had just gotten home from the library with my two young children. My son, Christian, was four months old and asleep in his car seat, and my daughter, Rebecca, was four years old and asking to watch a show. I turned on the television and heard the shocking news and saw the terrifying images of planes flying into buildings. I watched for a while until my daughter said, "Mommy, can we please turn it off—those pictures are too scary." And so I did. I sat in the silence, trying to make sense of the senseless, wondering what to say to my daughter. My husband called to check on us and to say that he would be late because he and other teachers at his school would accompany the students on their buses to make sure that their parents who worked in NYC were not among those killed, leaving an empty house. As I prayed for the children, I also prayed for pastors. As I secretly gave thanks that I was not serving a church at the time, I wondered what in the world preachers would say in their sermons on Sunday to the throngs who would surely go to church needing to hear a word of steadfast hope.

In troubled times, we turn to the trusted words of Scripture. There we find the words of Ecclesiastes, "For everything there is a season . . . a time to kill, and a time to heal . . . a time for war, and a time for peace" (vv. 1, 3, 8). Surely on 9/11 and at times of other local and national crises, world tragedies, and wars since, we are painfully aware of what has been killed, including people, security, and peace. There is a time to grieve the people and things that have been killed. At the same time, as ministers of the word, we must help people begin to heal and find peace, trusting that there is "a time for every matter under heaven."

One such matter is captured by a beautiful Hebrew phrase: *tikkun olam*. The phrase literally means "world repair" and is usually interpreted as meaning "to heal the world." It comes from the Mishnah, a third-century CE compilation of rabbinic teachings, and has inspired the obligation inherent in the Jewish faith to participate with God in repairing or healing the world through acts of kindness and social justice. If we believe that God is the creator of and ruler over all things, then we can affirm that God wills good and healing for all creation throughout all the times of life. Some are moments of crisis, when we cry out to God in despair and helplessness; some are moments of resolve, when we seek God's help as we pursue peace, justice, and the renewal of creation. All are moments of hope and possibility, as we remember that we are not alone as we seek healing for ourselves and our broken but beautiful world.

Even as we participate with God in the "healing of world," our individual hearts are broken and in need of healing. The Hebrew word *shalom* means peace and harmony, health and wholeness, safety and tranquility. At the beginning of the Sabbath, Jews exchange the greeting "Shabbat shalom" as a blessing, meaning, "May you dwell in peace on this Sabbath day, being in harmony with Yahweh." Similarly, many Christian worship services include a time for "passing the peace." During this time—as a greeting, a prayer, a charge, and a blessing—people say to one another, "Peace be with you." And in return, they say, "And also with you." Peace is not something that can or should be kept to oneself; instead, it must be passed on, toward the end of killing and war and the beginning of healing and peace. God's peace. Shalom.

With baptisms, weddings, and even funerals, a preacher usually has several months or at least a few days to write a sermon to preach for the occasion. But crises do not fit into our schedules. They are by nature disruptive and come unexpectedly, demanding our immediate attention and our pastoral response. As a pastor, you have no doubt found yourself in a similar situation—or if not, you will someday—when you need to say something in response to a local, national, or worldwide tragedy. This might include fires, floods, or other natural disasters; a global pandemic; or Russia's invasion of Ukraine and killing of innocent civilians. You might witness our country at war or the Capitol under the siege of an insurrection. A local crisis might present itself as poisoned water (Flint, MI); an anti-Semitic gunman killing Jews at the Tree of Life Synagogue (Pittsburgh, PA) or a racist gunman targeting and killing Black people at a grocery store (Buffalo, NY); wildfires destroying communities (Greenville, CA); an apartment blaze killing nineteen people, including nine children (Bronx, NYC); or a gunman's assault on an elementary school, killing two teachers and nineteen children (Uvalde, TX). Whatever the crisis, in the face of such overwhelming news, it is difficult to know what to think, let alone what to say.

What, then, shall we say about these things? For those of you who have been reading this book, you are familiar with the process of crafting a relevant sermon for an occasion within or outside of an ordinary Sunday. But if you just opened to this chapter because a crisis hit, and you need to know what to say in the face of a tragedy, this process of finding the words to preach begins with naming the contextual situation (What is going on here?), then identifying the congregation (Who is listening?), and finally, asking theological questions (Where is God?). This process will lead you from the crisis to the crafting of a sermon, from not knowing what to say toward finding a healing word for a broken people. Even in the midst of catastrophic events that leave us speechless, this process will help you preach a sermonic word that offers God's *shalom* and reveals God's plan of *tikkun olam* and our place in the healing of the world.

What Is Going On?

For people who have experienced a tragedy resulting in a significant loss in their lives, it can feel like the world is closing in on them, squeezing the life out of their spirit. These times cannot be avoided. Sometimes they just happen, as is witnessed in Ecclesiastes: there is "a time to kill," and there is "a time for war." Indeed, "for everything there is a season."

The season that began in March 2020 was a particularly challenging time of tragedy. On Friday, March 13, 2020, the World Health Organization declared a global pandemic. Cases of Covid-19 around the world were staggering, cases in our country were rising, and the first cases were reported in our own county in Pittsburgh, causing businesses to close. I called our church task force and session, and together we decided, out of an abundance of caution, to close the church building and only worship online. Little did we know of how long we would be closed, how long we would be at war with this virus, and how many millions of people would die worldwide.

On Monday, April 27, 2020, Hurricane Laura made landfall near Cameron, Louisiana, as a category four hurricane with a ten-foot-high storm surge, causing severe flooding and extreme damage to houses and killing forty-two people in its path. The hurricane had already hit Puerto Rico, the Dominican Republic, and Haiti, killing thirty-five people. Overall, Hurricane Laura caused more than $19.1 billion in damage and eighty-one deaths.

On Monday, May 26, 2020, breaking news reported that the day before, George Floyd had died after a Minneapolis police officer knelt on his neck for eight minutes and forty-six seconds (the time was revised during the trial to nine minutes and twenty-two seconds), suffocating him, despite his repeated pleas: "I can't breathe." In the following days, people responded by taking to the streets in protest, carrying "Black Lives Matter" signs and demanding justice and an end to the racial disparity in police shootings and to the disproportionate number of Black people being killed. In this season, just three months' time, it seemed as if the world was closing in on people, crushing their faith and hope and even threatening their very lives.

Using words of Scripture, ritual, prayer, and sermons, pastors relentlessly work to renew people's faith and restore their hope with the promise of *shalom*, encouraging them to join in the herculean effort to repair the world (*tikkun olam*). But when a pandemic, hurricane, inhumane death—or all three—simultaneously happen, we might feel like the person who plugs up a hole in a dike just as another leak breaks through. Soon, we realize that we cannot keep up with the leaks. Then what do we do? As pastors, we stand in the gap between the reality of the pain and the promise of the resurrection, often praying with sighs too deep for words.

But as preachers, we are called to speak. In times of crisis, we must find a voice to acknowledge the reality that the world is broken, even as we proclaim the truth that God is working to bring healing, as attested by the prophet Jeremiah: "For I will restore health to you, and your wounds I will heal, says the Lord" (30:17). To begin with, we name the pain. In the case of the pandemic, we name the number of infections and the losses on many levels. In the case of the hurricane, we name the power of nature that has been compromised by climate change. In the case of the death of George Floyd, we name the systemic racial injustice that allowed Floyd's death along with the deaths of Breonna Taylor, Ahmaud Arbery, Anthony Alvarez, Sean Monterrosa, and countless other people of color. We name the reality of the pain, even as we ask the question "What then are we to say about these things?" Before we rush to answer, we may need to sit with people in silence, listening to what they have to say—even if they speak in anger or despair or desolation, feeling that they have been abandoned by God. We need to be willing to sit in the unresolved tension, listening to what word people most need to hear us preach in the face of the unfathomable.

As you sit in the silence, wondering what to preach in a crisis, consider the context. Even though tragedies do not allow a lot of time to investigate and reflect, try to understand what is going on in these moments. Think about the physical setting. Where will you be preaching? Will you be preaching to an empty sanctuary in front of a camera to a virtual congregation quarantined at home? Will it be in a town ravaged by a hurricane? Will you be at a protest on the street or at a rally for justice on a front lawn? Will you be in a sanctuary following a shooting in a nearby church? The place where you stand will inform what you preach.

Most often, you will preach to your congregation, who may or may not be directly impacted by the current crisis. However, they will still gather seeking a word of acknowledgment and assurance of God's promise to be with us always: "When you pass through the waters, I will be with you; and through the rivers, they shall not overwhelm you" (Isa 43:2). I still remember a major flood that occurred in Findlay, Ohio, when I was serving a church there. On the following Sunday, I did not mention the flood in my sermon. It was already written, and as a new pastor and new parent, I just could not figure out how to make the time to write a new sermon on Saturday. Following worship, one church member challenged me, wondering how I could neglect to mention such a catastrophic event in the life of the community. Her chastisement was well deserved, and I have remembered it throughout my years of ministry. Lesson learned: give voice to the people's pain, even if you don't have an answer for it.

As you prepare for worship following a tragedy, consider the contextual issues that shape this occasion. What is the history of this event? Is it an ongoing issue? If so, why? How has your church been involved in this tragedy? Recounting the history can put the current crisis in perspective, helping listeners remember that people before us survived similar challenges, and so will we—and we may be called to prevent future ones. Giving witness to your congregational and/or denominational response to crises is also important, whether it be a pandemic call to action, a disaster-relief fund, or a commitment to racial justice.

Consider the liturgical and musical settings. You do not have to reinvent the wheel, so consult your denomination or other clergy colleagues to find liturgical resources such as prayers and hymns. Pay careful attention to how the liturgy can be used to name the pain and bring healing, to give space to the communal lament, and to offer prayers of peace. Be careful not to rush to tie up theological bows too quickly but instead to provide the words and rituals so people can express their lament. We are in good company with the psalmist and with believers throughout the centuries, who at different times and seasons have cried out:

How long, O Lord? Will you forget me forever?
　　How long will you hide your face from me?
How long must I bear pain in my soul,
　　and have sorrow in my heart all day long?
How long shall my enemy be exalted over me?
　　(Ps 13:1–2)

As you craft the liturgy, select hymns that give voice to the sorrow and longing people feel deeply. Before you ask worshippers to sing with confidence, "Jesus loves me, this I know," allow them to sing, "There is a longing in our hearts, O God, for you to reveal yourself to us."[1]

Let the prayers echo the message of the sermon. On the Sunday after the killing of George Floyd, for the prayers of the people, I knelt in the chancel and invited people at home (via livestream) to join me, and there I stayed in silence on my knees for eight minutes and forty-six seconds, emphasizing the officer's excessive and fatal use of force. Lord, in your mercy, hear our prayer.

When preachers stand or kneel in the liminal space between heartbreak and hope, between pain and promise with and for their congregations, they are not afraid to testify that yes, indeed, the world is broken—not in panic but in proclamation of the truth. It is important to remember ourselves and remind our listeners that life happens and that mystery abounds. Do not say more than you know, but do not be afraid to say what you do know: that God does not cause the brokenness; instead, God's heart is broken when tragedy strikes. God does not create the crises; rather, God cries in the face of pain and sorrow. God does not rejoice in wrongdoing; God rejoices in the truth. What is going on? Even if you struggle to understand it, Scripture gives us words that are trusted and true:

Thus says the Lord . . .
I am about to do a new thing;
   now it springs forth, do you not perceive it?
I will make a way in the wilderness
   and rivers in the desert. (Isa 43:19)

As we contemplate what to say in our sermons, we start with wondering, "What is going on in this crisis?" Even as we name the pain and testify to the truths that there is "a time to kill" and there is "a time for war," we begin to look ahead and around, look up and within, seeking to find "a time to heal" and "a time for peace." We do so trusting that in God's time, there is "a time for every matter under heaven."

Who Is Listening?

"Know your audience," speakers and writers are told, so that your message has a better chance of connecting with them. The same counsel is given to preachers. In seminary, we are taught not only to exegete a biblical text for meaning but also to exegete the congregation—who they are, why they are coming to church, and what they are hoping to experience in worship and hear in the sermon.[2] Before you read a biblical text, but after you have identified the issue, consider your listeners. Some will come to church hoping to hear you address current events from the pulpit; others will come with their fingers in their ears, wishing you would stick to sacred speech about heavenly promises, not earthly problems. You will find people on both sides of any political divide: those who trust the science and others who think the pandemic is a hoax; those who think that catastrophic weather patterns are the result of climate change and those who see no evidence; those who support police officers without question and those who do not feel that all people are equally protected by them and must protest for justice for all. In the same pew will be people who wonder why the church doesn't do more to make a public witness to help right the wrongs of the world and others who come seeking solace, sanctuary, and silence. On any given Sunday, in any given church, you can bet some people hunger for justice and righteousness and others are hungry only for lunch.

But what matters is your particular congregation. So take time to imagine your listeners, why they come to worship, and what they hope to hear. Sometimes, it helps to go into the sanctuary or the place they will gather and picture them. Most people sit in the same pew Sunday after Sunday, year after year, so you can easily bring them to mind. As you look around the church, stop at each pew and ask yourself, "What are they thinking and wondering about this tragedy? What are they feeling?" If you give yourself time to imagine, you will recognize much pain among your people. And to the pain you are aware of, you can add even more that has not been shared but that based on people's behavior, you know is there. Likely, most people in the pews will have experienced "a time to kill" and a "time for war" during which they have suffered the death of something dear to them, perhaps leaving a wound that is hard to heal. In *Words That Heal: Preaching Hope to Wounded Souls*, homiletician Joni Sancken calls these experiences of suffering from personal trauma or abuse or loss "soul wounds." In addition, Sancken claims, "Some soul wounds are rooted in a national event—those who have survived a mass shooting or those for whom the news coverage of the most recent national tragedy triggers memories of a violent experience in their own lives."[3] Because these wounds are often hidden deep within, it is difficult for preachers to attend to them, but even so, it is essential that they do so.

How do we attend to the "soul wounds" that our listeners bear? First, we have to consider what they might be. Think about the people in your congregation. I think of Teresa, who is angry with those who do not wear masks. Deep inside, she is grieving the death of her father from Covid-19, who was likely exposed at church. For some, like Teresa, a calamity like the coronavirus pandemic threatens their faith. Trust is compromised with suspicion that those around you may not be vaccinated. Such overwhelming tragedies trouble the mind as people cry out in the words of the psalmist:

> I wait for the Lord, my soul waits,
>> and in his word I hope;
> my soul waits for the Lord
>> more than those who watch for the morning,
>> more than those who watch for the morning.
>> (Ps 130:5–6)

As I look around my congregation, I wonder if Sam is sick with worry about people who are homeless after the hurricane, remembering losing all his belongings in a flood years ago. For some, like Sam, catastrophic storms threaten to drown their hopes that the sun will come out tomorrow. Fear has multiplied exponentially and amplified a sense of vulnerability. Such natural catastrophes trouble the spirit as people pray,

> Be merciful to me, O God, be merciful to me,
>> for in you my soul takes refuge;
> in the shadow of your wings, I will take refuge,
>> until the destroying storms pass by. (Ps 57:1)

I see Henry as a Black man supporting protests for racial justice following the death of George Floyd, and I wonder if he is fearful for his teenage boys, recalling his own painful memories of police brutality. For some, like Henry, such a racially charged killing can rightly harden hearts and surface distrust that chokes off relationships between people, communities, racial groups, and God. Such tragedies trouble the heart as people take up the chorus of the persecuted:

> I say to God, my rock,
>> "Why have you forgotten me?
> Why must I walk about mournfully
>> because the enemy oppresses me?"
> As with a deadly wound in my body,
>> my adversaries taunt me,
> while they say to me continually,
>> "Where is your God?" (Ps 42:9–10)

Tragic events happen, giving witness to the truth that there is a time to kill and a time for war. Following a tragedy, those who gather in church to listen to a sermon come from many different places, at times carrying heavy burdens, bearing deep soul wounds. Some come with minds troubled by fear. Others come with spirits disturbed by despair. Still others come with hearts hardened by anger. And no matter the disturbance, people feel it in their bodies, and their sense of peace is in peril.

When we consider who will be listening to our sermon and what soul wounds they bear, we as pastors are moved to compassion. The literal meaning of *compassion* is "to suffer with" someone. Joni Sancken reveals the deeply visceral connotation of the

Hebrew word for compassion, *rachamim*, with the root word *rechem*, meaning "womb." She credits theologian Andrew Purves for his significant work in defining the literal meaning of compassion as "the womb pained in solidarity with the suffering of another." That is to say, "God's womb aches when God's people suffer."[4] And as the people of God, we all ache together. These are the listeners who come to church, seeking what they might not even be able to name but hoping that they can find a much-needed balm for soul wounds in need of healing. By listening to the wounded listeners in our midst, we become aware of the brokenness in our world and are compelled to tell the truth about it, even as we are unsure about what to say.

Pastors are keenly aware of the wounds of their listeners but not always willing to admit that they themselves are wounded. As pastors, we often "mask" our wounds. But if we open them up, even if just in our study time, prayer time, or therapy sessions, we allow ourselves to be vulnerable and better able to connect with our listeners. If we can examine and name our own wounds, they can be transformed from weakness to strength. As we honestly accept and live into our calling as wounded healers, we can offer healing words of *shalom* to our listeners and be a part of *tikkun olam*.

Our part in the healing of the world begins with helping to heal wounded souls. Our calling is to preach but first to be present with those who suffer. When someone calls saying, "There's been an accident, can you come?"; when the text reads, "The hospice nurse says it won't be long, can you come?"; when the mourner walks toward the grave with dirt in her hand, asking, "Can you come?" the answer is yes every time. Of course, I will come. And I will stand with you. Yes. That's what we pastors do. We go with. We stand with. We stay with. We pray with.

The value of pastoral presence cannot be underestimated, especially in tragic times. And although there is a time to be silent in the face of such mystery, there is also a time to speak. At the hospital, at the hospice center, at the grave, after the silence, we need to speak. As ministers of the word, we are called to speak a word of promise into a world of pain, a word of compassion into a world of crisis, a word of truth into a world of trauma, a word of grace into a world of gravitas. What language shall we borrow? As you think about preaching, consider who might be listening to your sermon and what they might be listening for. People who come seeking a time to heal and a time for peace are listening for a word of grace, even hoping for a glimpse of God.

Where Is God?

After you have thought about the context and the congregation, you then need to consider the theological issues at the heart of the matter, especially the hardest but most important question of all: If God is all good and all powerful, then why is there suffering in the world? It is the question of theodicy that serves as an atheist's "get out of church free card." It is the question that gets caught in the throat of an earnest believer who has been cut to the heart by a harrowing loss. It is the question that preachers avoid asking in sermons, because they know full well they do not have an adequate answer with which to assuage their listeners, let alone themselves. Homiletician Tom Long claims that trying to answer the theodicy question and balance the equation of a good and powerful God and an evil world is a chess match that we cannot win. In *What Shall We Say? Evil, Suffering, and the Crisis of Faith*, Long challenges preachers to take seriously the theodicy dilemma and adeptly guides readers to a faithful resolution we can preach with integrity. To do so, Long examines the parable of the wheat and the weeds:

> Jesus put before them another parable: "The kingdom of heaven may be compared to someone who sowed good seed in his field; but while everybody was asleep, an enemy came and sowed weeds among the wheat, and then went away. So when the plants came up and bore grain, then the weeds appeared as well. And the slaves of the householder came and said to him, 'Master, did you not sow good seed in your field? Where, then, did these weeds come from?' He answered, 'An enemy has done this.' The slaves said to him, 'Then do you want us to go and gather them?' But he replied, 'No; for in gathering the weeds you would uproot the wheat along with them. Let both of them grow together until the harvest; and at harvest time I will tell the reapers, 'Collect the weeds first and bind them in bundles to be burned, but gather the wheat into my barn.'" (Matt 13:24–30)

Long interprets this parable as a pastoral conversation about the presence of good and evil in the world, in which he imagines people asking the pastor three urgent questions: "God, did you cause this? Can we fix it? Will it always be this way?"

God, Did You Cause This?
In the parable, the servants go to the master of the house and ask, "Did you not sow good seed in your field? Where, then, did these evil weeds come from?" The servants demand to know how this could have happened. They rightly wonder, "Did you cause this?" Long claims this is the first insight from

this parable: "The gospel enables and empowers the raised fist of protest."[5] That is to say, the gospel does not minimize the presence of evil or let God off the hook—for an infant who dies in the crib, an earthquake that destroys a town, a woman who is raped on her way home from work, or a suicide bomb that kills troops and civilians at an airport. It allows one to raise a fist heavenward and demand an answer.

Long relates the story of a physician who told him, "When I get to heaven—*if* I get to heaven—I'm going to go directly to the throne room of God with a cancer cell in my hand and say, 'Why?'" Long argues that this theodicy of protest "is the visceral response of people who trust God and feel betrayed."[6] Joni Sancken claims that anger has a place—and it is with God: "God does not need our protection. Anger at God can be a natural and helpful response to trauma and can maintain and even energize relationship. God is large enough to receive our anger, to safely and securely hold it so that it doesn't harm others or us."[7]

The ultimate example of theodicy protest in the Bible is from Job, who was "blameless and upright, one who feared God and turned away from evil" (Job 1:1), and yet Satan destroyed everything he had and everyone he loved. Job protested, "I loathe my life; I will give free utterance to my complaint; I will speak in the bitterness of my soul. I will say to God, Do not condemn me; let me know why you contend against me" (Job 10:1–2). Why? Like Job, the psalmist cries out in protest and demands an answer: "My God, my God, why have you forsaken me? Why are you so far from helping me, from the words of my groaning?" (Ps 22:1). Although necessary and right, the parable, the psalm, and Job do not stop with protest, and neither can we. We need to understand. Why?

In the parable, to the servant's demand for an answer as to why the field was corrupted by evil weeds, the landowner answers, "An enemy has done this." This simple answer has significant implications. First, the landowner is making clear that he is not the source of the weeds; that is to say, "evil is God's enemy. Not God's instrument, not God's counterpart, not something about which God is indifferent. Evil is God's enemy, period."[8] This evil is a force in the world and in the human heart. Evil in any form—the evil that takes the life of an infant, destroys a town, rapes a woman, or kills innocent bystanders—is our enemy and God's enemy too.

Scripture from both testaments bears witness to this truth. The wisdom of Proverbs testifies, "The fear of the Lord is hatred of evil" (8:13); "The way of the Lord is a stronghold for the upright, but destruction for evildoers" (10:29); "Deceit is in the mind of those who plan evil, but those who counsel peace have joy. No harm happens to the righteous, but the wicked are filled with trouble" (12:21).

The apostle Paul instructs the early churches on the battle with evil:

> Finally, be strong in the Lord and in the strength of his power. Put on the whole armor of God, so that you may be able to stand against the wiles of the devil. For our struggle is not against enemies of blood and flesh, but against the rulers, against the authorities, against the cosmic powers of this present darkness, against the spiritual forces of evil in the heavenly places. Therefore, take up the whole armor of God, so that you may be able to withstand on that evil day, and having done everything, to stand firm. (Eph 6:10–13)

In the face of tragedy, people come to church with this question on their minds but are afraid to speak it, "God, did you cause this?" A preacher is able to ask this difficult question on behalf of his people. And once the question is spoken aloud, the preacher will have the full attention of her people as she seeks to answer it.

Can We Fix It?

After the landowner in the parable declares that he did not cause the evil weeds, but the enemy did, the servants ask, "Then do you want us to go and gather them?" In other words, they are asking, "Should we go and pluck out the evil and leave the good? Can we fix it?" The landowner replies, "No; for in gathering the weeds you would uproot the wheat along with them." This answer recognizes the perniciousness of evil and the limited power of human beings. Long states, "The servants are forbidden to run roughshod into the field, plucking up the weeds, not only because they lack the wisdom to do so without damaging the wheat, but also because *this is not God's way in the world*."[9] What is God's way? we wonder. If God hates evil, then why doesn't God obliterate all evildoers? Long posits that the truth lies in God's character:

> What if God does come as a warrior, but not as a warrior who fights like a human combatant, but as a warrior God who fights only with weapons of love? God is indeed all-powerful, but God's power is not like raw human power but is instead a love that takes the form of weakness, a power expressed most dramatically on the cross. We think we want God to plunge into creation with a machete and to slash away at evil. It is not that this

is somehow out of God's range of power; it is that this kind of power is out of God's range of character.[10]

Our Christian faith is based on a belief in the power of God—to create, to part waters, to provide manna, to make covenant, to return from exile, to keep promises, to become flesh. God's character is most clearly and powerfully seen on the cross:

- Jesus says, "No one has greater love than this, to lay down one's life for one's friends" (John 15:13).
- "Then Jesus gave a loud cry and breathed his last. And the curtain of the temple was torn in two, from top to bottom. Now when the centurion, who stood facing him, saw that in this way he breathed his last, he said, 'Truly this man was God's Son!'" (Mark 15:37–39).
- Paul instructed the disciples of Jesus to live in this way: "Do not by overcome by evil, but overcome evil with good" (Rom 12:21).
- "For the message about the cross is foolishness to those who are perishing, but to us who are being saved, it is the power of God" (1 Cor 1:18).

These Scripture passages testify to the breadth and depth of God's love in the birth, life, death, and resurrection of Jesus Christ. Our sermons do not promise that we can fix the problems of the world by ourselves, but they testify that God is always at work, trying to bring good out of evil, life out of death.

Will It Always Be This Way?

The answer the parable provides is an unequivocal no. The landowner says, "At harvest time, I will tell the reapers, 'Collect the weeds first and bind them in bundles to be burned, but gather the wheat into my barn.'" This makes it clear that although evil and good will grow together, in the end, God will separate them and will have the last word of justice and love. Long describes the inherent paradox: "The love of God, seemingly so weak on the cross, ends up victorious and ultimately destroys the power of evil. . . . The nonviolence of God's love ultimately does violence to evil. The Prince of Peace is, in regard to cosmic evil, the divine warrior."[11]

So then, how is a pastor to answer the questions of theodicy that the people will ask directly or indirectly through their fear, despair, anger, or absence? A genuine Christian response must bear witness to the fact that suffering and evil are enemies of God and that God is a warrior whose power is love, most fully revealed on the cross. As pastors, we stand in the pain with wounded people and at the same time witness to the promise that death will be swallowed up, and a time will come when God "will wipe every tear from their eyes. Death will be no more; mourning and crying and pain will be no more, for the first things have passed away" (Rev 21:4).

These are powerful words of God's ultimate promise to defeat evil for good and make all things right in the end of time. But what about the time in which we live, when we face tragedies in this life, when evil has its way, when we experience a time to kill and a time for war? For people who come to church following a personal or national crisis that troubles their minds, spirits, and hearts and threatens their faith, hope, love, and peace, how does a preacher name grace in troubled times?

Preachers are called to stand in the midst of the congregation in times of warring factions that kill the body, mind, and spirit and preach that in "a time to kill," there is "a time to heal"; in "a time for war," there is "a time for peace." Into the bad news of the world, preachers courageously preach the good news—that "[God] has made everything suitable for its time." Where can we find this good news? One need look no further than the Bible. Here are some Scripture passages that reveal the truth of the God of Promises and the Prince of Peace:

To inspire faith for troubled minds

Psalm 46 "God is our refuge and strength,
a very present help in trouble.
Therefore, we will not fear . . .
Be still and know that I am God! . . .
The Lord of hosts is with us;
the God of Jacob is our refuge."

Hebrews 11:1 "Now faith is the assurance of things hoped for, the conviction of things not seen."

Hebrews 12:3 "Consider him who endured such hostility against himself from sinners, so that you may not grow weary or lose heart."

To imbue hope for troubled souls

Psalm 42:5 "Why are you cast down, O my soul,
and why are you disquieted within me?
Hope in God; for I shall again praise him,
my help and my God."

Romans 5:1–5 "We also boast in our sufferings, knowing that suffering produces endurance, and endurance produces character, and character produces hope, and hope does not disappoint us, because God's love has been poured into our hearts through the Holy Spirit that has been given to us."

Romans 8:22–23 "For in hope we were saved. Now hope that is seen is not hope. For who hopes for what is seen? But if we hope for what we do not see, we wait for it with patience."

To instill love for troubled hearts

Isaiah 43:1–5 "But now thus says the Lord . . .

'Do not fear, for I have redeemed you;
I have called you by name, you are mine . . .
Because you are precious in my sight,
and honored, and I love you. . . .
Do not fear, for I am with you.'"

Romans 8:31–39 "For I am convinced that neither death nor life, nor angels, nor rulers, nor things present, nor things to come, nor powers, nor height, nor depth, nor anything else in all creation, will be able to separate us from the love of God in Christ Jesus our Lord."

1 Corinthians 13:12–13 "For now we see in a mirror, but then we will see face to face. Now I know only in part; then I will know fully, even as I have been fully known. And now faith, hope, and love abide, these three; and the greatest of these is love."

To imagine peace in troubled times

John 14:26–27   "Peace I leave with you; my peace I give to you. I do not give to you as the world gives. Do not let your hearts be troubled, and do not let them be afraid."

Philippians 4:6–7   "Do not worry about anything, but in everything by prayer and supplication with thanksgiving let your requests be made known to God. And the peace of God, which surpasses all understanding, will guard your hearts and your minds in Christ Jesus."

These Scripture verses give witness to the promises of our faith. And we, as preachers, are called to stand in the pulpit and preach a sermon in which we not only interpret the biblical text but also testify to what we believe it says to people today. We name the grace that we hear God speaking into the gravitas today. We give witness to the truth that God did not cause the crisis; God is at work trying to fix it—or at least bring some good out of it. And no, it will not always be this way. Thanks be to God.

In the end, this is what preachers are called to do—no more and no less than to give witness to what they have seen in the world and heard in Scripture and believe to be true. The preacher's witness is how the message of God's presence in the midst of crisis and tragedy is conveyed. In her book *Spirit and Trauma: A Theology of Remaining*, theologian Shelly Rambo details the power of witness in the face of trauma. She writes about Holocaust survivor and author Elie Wiesel, who has witnessed mass atrocities. Wiesel traces the development of a new genre of literature: "If the Greeks invented tragedy, the Romans the epistle, and the Renaissance the sonnet, our generation invented a new literature, that of testimony."[12] Rambo argues for the essential role of a witness to trauma—testifying to that which has been killed and to that which can be healed—as their witness "takes into account the depth to which human persons can be shattered and it equally takes into account the important work of remaking the world."[13] *Tikkun olam.* Witness, claims Rambo, "is the hinge linking the shattering and remaking, the undoing and the regeneration. Witness is the hinge between death and life."[14] In the aftermath of a tragedy, pastors are called to stand in the midst of the trauma, at the hinge between life and death. Here, we cannot prove anything. We cannot take away the pain. We cannot speed up the time until the realization of God's promise that there will be no more mourning or crying and death shall be no more. All we can do is stand with the mourners in their trauma and give authentic witness to the power of healing in and through it. We do this with our comforting presence and in our courageous proclamation. And even if we cannot preach like Peter or pray like Paul, we can tell the love of Jesus and witness to the truth that there is a balm in God's word to heal the wounded soul.

I will never forget the funeral I did on my son's third birthday. We would be celebrating later in the day, but first, I had to stand with a mother who was burying her twenty-three-year-old son. The sanctuary was full of church members, community members, and people whose faith was shaken to the core. Etched on their sunken faces and spilling out of their forlorn eyes, I could see the question: "If God is powerful and good, then why did this happen?" I stood in the church and read Scripture ("In life and in death we belong to God"). I proclaimed

("Nothing—not our questions or our fears, not our anger or our tears—nothing will be able to separate us from the love of God in Christ Jesus our Lord"). I prayed ("You are nearest to us when we need you most. In this hour of sorrow, we turn to you, not sure what else to do but to trust in your loving mercy"). And I blessed them ("Now may the peace of God, which surpasses all understanding, guard your hearts and minds in Christ Jesus").

After the funeral, we went to the cemetery for the committal service. I recited the words that Jesus said to Martha at the tomb of her brother Lazarus, promising her, "Your brother will rise again" and "I am the resurrection and the life. Those who believe in me, even though they die, will live, and everyone who lives and believes in me will never die" (John 11:25–26).

Afterward, just like Jesus asked Martha, the mother whose son we buried asked me, "Do you believe this? Will my son rise from the dead? Will I see my son again in heaven? Do you really believe it is true?" I realized that what she needed most in this hour of grief was a witness. I looked at her, and as I choked back the tears, I witnessed, "Yes, I believe. I believe in the promises of our faith. I believe in the resurrection to eternal life. I believe in a God who loves the world so much that he gave his only son, who died and rose again for your son and for you and all of us. I believe it's true. It's the truest thing I know. And I will believe for you until you can believe again."

One week after the twentieth anniversary of the catastrophic events of September 11, 2001, my husband and I took a trip to the Flight 93 National Memorial outside Shanksville, Pennsylvania, where one of the hijacked airplanes crashed, killing all forty people aboard. We experienced the monument, museum, and field as a place of both horror and healing, a place of pain and peace. As we walked around the large, open field, we came upon a sign that gave a powerful witness:

> Flight 93 National Memorial is a place of renewal. It embraces the natural environment, both stark and serene. Land scarred by decades of coal mining is being restored. Native trees are once again part of the landscape, and flowering meadows soften remnants of the area's harsh industrial past. Wetlands filter the water and create a habitat teeming with life. With time, this landscape will be transformed by nature, just as this place was changed by the events of September 11, 2001.

For everything there is a season and a time for every matter under heaven. There is a time to kill and a time to heal. A time for war and a time for peace.

A BENEDICTION

[God] has made everything suitable for its time.
—Ecclesiastes 3:11

March 15, 2020, was no ordinary Sunday. The World Health Organization had just declared Covid-19 a worldwide pandemic, and the Centers for Disease Control had just recommended, based on the alarming infection rate, that states close businesses, schools, and churches. Donna preached to an empty sanctuary and an online congregation that Sunday. The question the apostle Paul asked in his letter to the Romans guided her sermon: "What then are we to say about these things?" (Rom 8:31). Her answer was "Lean in," even in a time of shock, fear, sorrow, and social distancing. "Lean in. Lean in to God's everlasting promises and abiding presence. Lean in to God's mighty power and deep peace. Lean in to God's loving arms. Lean in to God, in whom we belong, in life and in death. Because nothing will be able to separate us from the love of God in Christ Jesus our Lord."

As the preacher of Ecclesiastes wisely reminds us, "For everything there is a season, and a time for every matter under heaven." For everything there is a season—a time to be born and a time to die . . . a time to kill and a time to heal . . . a time to mourn and a time to dance . . . a time to keep silence and a time to speak. And as we learned in 2020, there is even a time for a pandemic. As all preachers have learned, many different times arise in ministry—some expectedly and some unexpectedly—that call for a word from the Lord. In ordinary and extraordinary times and every time in between, like Moses and Esther and Paul and so many before us, preachers are called to proclaim a word that reminds our listeners there is a time for every matter under heaven. But it is often in those times, when we are unsure of what to say, that we have to speak. We may hold deep in our hearts the resurrection hope that death does not have the last word—God does, and it is a word of life, abundant and eternal life. But how do we capture the hopes and fears of the people and give voice to a sermon that proclaims, in no uncertain terms, God's promise to be with us always?

If you are reading this conclusion, then you have probably already read the introduction that lays out our process for moving from the context of a special occasion to a scriptural text. Or maybe you only read the chapter(s) that would help you prepare to preach for a specific out-of-the-ordinary occasion. Either way, by now, you are familiar with our process: start with the occasion, asking, "What is going on?" Then think about those who will be gathered before you, asking, "Who is listening?" Finally, consider the theological issues surrounding the occasion, asking, "Where is God?" Thoughtful and prayerful reflection on each of these questions will lead you to selecting Scripture passages. Now, ready or not, it is time to craft the sermon. But you may still be wondering: how? How can you craft a sermon that is fitting to the context and occasion and faithful to the biblical text so that you can preach a relevant and redemptive word?

As longtime preachers ourselves, we say this: lean in. Lean in to the tension and anxiety. Lean in to the questions and considerations. Lean in to your call to preach. Lean in to the love you have for the people God has placed before you. Lean in to the truth of God's love that will not let us go. Lean in to Jesus's commission to go and teach and his promise to be with us always. Lean in to your faith that the Holy Spirit will guide and inspire you as you craft your sermon. Lean in to prayer to receive a word from God for the people of God. Lean in to the promise that God abides with us always, in every time and season.

Now lean in to crafting your sermon. Now is the time. You have done the hard and faithful work. Trust that the words will come, praying all the time, "Speak, Lord, for your people are listening." Do not be afraid, for the God who abides with us through every matter under heaven has made everything suitable for its time. May it be so.

Donna Giver-Johnston
Beverly Zink-Sawyer

NOTES

Chapter 1: From Context to Text

1 Jeremy Davies, *In Season and Out of Season: Crafting Sermons for All Occasions* (Norwich, UK: Canterbury, 2014), 161.

2 David J. Schlafer, *What Makes This Day Different? Preaching Grace on Special Occasions* (Lanham, MD: Rowman & Littlefield, 1998), 3. For more on defining and preaching on special occasions, see also Ronald J. Allen, *Preaching the Topical Sermon* (Louisville, KY: Westminster John Knox, 1992); and David Schnasa Jacobsen and Robert Allen Kelly, *Kairos Preaching: Speaking Gospel to the Situation* (Minneapolis: Fortress, 2009).

3 Marvin A. McMickle, *Living Water for Thirsty Souls: Unleashing the Power of Exegetical Preaching* (Valley Forge, PA: Judson, 2001), 174.

4 David Buttrick, *Homiletic: Moves and Structures* (Minneapolis: Fortress, 1987), 405.

5 Buttrick, 405.

6 James C. Howell, *The Beauty of the Word: The Challenge and Wonder of Preaching* (Louisville, KY: Westminster John Knox, 2011), 13.

7 Cleophus LaRue, *The Heart of Black Preaching* (Louisville, KY: Westminster John Knox, 2000), 123.

8 Eunjoo Mary Kim, *Preaching the Presence of God: A Homiletic from an Asian American Perspective* (Valley Forge, PA: Judson, 1999), 2.

9 Leonora Tubbs Tisdale, *Preaching as Local Theology and Folk Art* (Minneapolis: Fortress, 1997), xii.

10 Richard Lischer, *The End of Words: The Language of Reconciliation in a Culture of Violence* (Grand Rapids, MI: Eerdmans, 2005), 57.

11 Mary Catherine Hilkert, *Naming Grace: Preaching and the Sacramental Imagination* (New York: Continuum, 1997), 44.

12 Hilkert, 46.

13 Karoline M. Lewis, *A Lay Preacher's Guide: How to Craft a Faithful Sermon* (Minneapolis: Fortress, 2020), 63.

14 Lewis, 62.

15 Buttrick, *Homiletic*, 425.

16 Barbara Brown Taylor, *The Preaching Life* (Lanham, MD: Rowman & Littlefield, 1993), 58.

17 Lischer, *End of Words*, 57.

18 Howell, *Beauty of the Word*, 82.

19 Howell, 81.

20 Thomas G. Long, *The Witness of Preaching*, 3rd ed. (Louisville, KY: Westminster John Knox, 2016), 62.

21 Ellen F. Davis, *Wondrous Depth: Preaching the Old Testament* (Louisville, KY: Westminster John Knox, 2005), 4.

22 Howell, *Beauty of the Word*.

Chapter 2: Baptisms

1 *Book of Common Worship* (Louisville, KY: Westminster John Knox, 2018), 408.

2 Rowan Williams, *Being Christian: Baptism, Bible, Eucharist, Prayer* (Grand Rapids, MI: Eerdmans, 2014), 5.

3 Gerald Liu and Khalia Williams, *A Worship Workbook: A Practical Guide for Extraordinary Liturgy* (Nashville: Abingdon, 2021), 37.

4 Herbert Anderson and Edward Foley, *Mighty Stories, Dangerous Rituals: Weaving Together the Human and the Divine* (San Francisco: Jossey-Bass, 1998), 65, 72.

5 James C. Howell, *The Beauty of the Word: The Challenge and Wonder of Preaching* (Louisville, KY: Westminster John Knox, 2011), 82.

6 Gail Ramshaw, *Christian Worship: 100,000 Sundays of Symbols and Rituals* (Minneapolis: Fortress, 2009), 147.

7 Thomas G. Long, *The Witness of Preaching*, 3rd ed. (Louisville, KY: Westminster John Knox, 2016), 54.

8 Ellen F. Davis, *Wondrous Depth: Preaching the Old Testament* (Louisville, KY: Westminster John Knox, 2005), 4.

9 Jana Childers, ed., *Birthing the Sermon: Women Preachers on the Creative Process* (St. Louis, MO: Chalice, 2001), ix.

Chapter 3: Funerals

1 Thomas G. Long, *Accompany Them with Singing: The Christian Funeral* (Louisville, KY: Westminster John Knox, 2009), 121.

2 Woody Allen, "Quote by Woody Allen: 'I'm Not Afraid of Death,'" Goodreads, accessed January 24, 2022, https://www.goodreads.com/quotes/2989-i-m-not-afraid-of-death-i-just-don-t-want-to.

3 Mark Twain, "Quote by Mark Twain: 'The Fear of Death Follows from the Fear of Life,'" Goodreads, accessed January 24, 2022, https://www.goodreads.com/quotes/5785-the-fear-of-death-follows-from-the-fear-of-life.

4 Herbert Anderson and Edward Foley, *Mighty Stories, Dangerous Rituals: Weaving Together the Human and the Divine* (San Francisco: Jossey-Bass, 1998), 100.

5 Steve Leder, *The Beauty of What Remains: How Our Greatest Fear Becomes Our Greatest Gift* (New York: Avery, 2021), 89.

6 Kalen Bruce, *10 Branches of Growth: Real-Life Productivity for a Fruitful Life* (n.p.: Kalen Bruce, 2020), 108.

7 Leder, *Beauty of What Remains*, 101.

8 *Book of Common Worship* (Louisville, KY: Westminster John Knox, 2018), 787–88.

9 Long, *Accompany Them with Singing*, 121.

10 Anderson and Foley, *Mighty Stories*, 115–16.

11 Anderson and Foley, 122.

12 Laurence Hull Stookey, *Calendar: Christ's Time for the Church* (Nashville: Abingdon, 1996), 17.

13 Long, *Accompany Them with Singing*, 187.

14 Henri J. M. Nouwen, *A Letter of Consolation* (San Francisco: HarperSanFrancisco, 1982), 16–17.

Chapter 4: Calls, Commissionings, and Commitments

1 Most denominations have books of occasional services that provide resources for worship and inspiration for sermons.

2 This section of the chapter refers primarily to those being ordained to ministry but can easily be adapted for both clergy and laity who are ordained, installed, consecrated, licensed, or otherwise set apart for leadership positions in the church.

3 William H. Willimon, *Pastor: The Theology and Practice of the Ordained Ministry* (Nashville: Abingdon, 2002), 16.

4 David J. Schlafer, *What Makes This Day Different? Preaching Grace on Special Occasions* (Lanham, MD: Rowman & Littlefield, 1998), 47.

5 Schlafer, 52.

6 Willimon, *Pastor*, 12, 15.

7 *Book of Common Worship* (Louisville, KY: Westminster John Knox, 2018), 467.

8 Schlafer, *What Makes This Day Different?*, 49.

9 Some denominations ordain church leaders such as elders and deacons.

10 See Garson O'Toole, "Blessed Are Those Who Plant Trees under Whose Shade They Will Never Sit," Quote Investigator, accessed February 28, 2022, https://quoteinvestigator.com/2020/04/29/tree -shade/.

Chapter 5: Congregational Conflicts, Closures, and Changes

1 David A. Roozen, *American Congregations 2010: A Decade of Change in American Congregations, 2000–2010* (Hartford, CT: Hartford Institute for Religion Research, 2011), 8.

2 David A. Roozen, *American Congregations 2015: Thriving and Surviving* (Hartford, CT: Hartford Institute for Religion Research, 2016), 7.

3 Leanna K. Fuller, *When Christ's Body Is Broken: Anxiety, Identity, and Conflict in Congregations* (Eugene, OR: Pickwick, 2016), 6.

4 Leanna K. Fuller, "A Splinter, Then a Crack: Leadership in the Aftermath of Divisive Conflict," *Journal of Religious Leadership* 20, no. 1 (Spring 2021): 115.

5 Joey Jeter Jr., quoting Andrew Lester from a lecture at Brite Divinity School, Fort Worth, TX, June 24, 1993, in *Crisis Preaching: Personal and Public* (Nashville: Abingdon, 1998), 18.

6 John S. McClure, "Preaching as a New Pastor in Times of Congregational Crisis," in *Transitions: Leading Churches through Change*, ed. David N. Mosser (Louisville, KY: Westminster John Knox, 2011), 197.

7 Taylor Billings Russell, "COVID-19 and Church Closures," United Church of Christ, Vital Signs and Statistics, November 9, 2020, https://carducc.wordpress.com/2020/11/09/covid-19-and-church-closures/.

8 Scott Thumma, *20 Years of Congregational Change: The 2020 Faith Communities Overview Today* (Hartford, CT: Hartford Institute for Religion Research, 2021), 13.

9 Jeffrey M. Jones, "U.S. Church Membership Falls Below Majority for First Time," *Gallup*, March 29, 2021, https://news.gallup.com/poll/341963/church-membership-falls-below-majority-first-time.aspx.

10 Beth Ann Gaede, ed., *Ending with Hope: A Resource for Closing Congregations* (Lanham, MD: Rowman & Littlefield, 2002), vii.

11 Thumma, *20 Years*, 23.

12 Beverly A. Thompson and George B. Thompson Jr., *Grace for the Journey: Practices and Possibilities for In-between Times* (Lanham, MD: Rowman & Littlefield, 2011), 3.

13 Prayer attributed to Reinhold Niebuhr.

14 Fuller, "Splinter, Then a Crack," 121. In her article, Fuller draws on the work of disaster ministry experts Laurie Kraus, David Holyan, and Bruce Wismer.

15 McClure, "Preaching as a New Pastor," 198.

16 Fuller, "Splinter, Then a Crack," 123.

17 Lisa M. Maddox, *Did God Abandon Us? Helping Small Churches Heal* (Cleveland, OH: Pilgrim, 2013), 61.

18 Gil Rendle, *Quietly Courageous: Leading the Church in a Changing World* (Lanham, MD: Rowman & Littlefield, 2019), 220.

19 Rendle, 249.

20 Fuller, "Splinter, Then a Crack," 127.

21 Leo S. Thorne, ed., *Prayers from Riverside* (New York: Pilgrim, 1983), 50.

22 McClure, "Preaching as a New Pastor," 200.

23 Comments were made by Rev. Dr. Sheldon Sorge in an interview at the Pittsburgh Presbytery Center on January 16, 2020.

24 James Baldwin, "The Blind Men and the Elephant," AmericanLiterature .com, accessed February 9, 2022, https://americanliterature.com/author/james-baldwin/short-story/the-blind-men-and-the-elephant.

Chapter 6: Older Adult Communities

1 This chapter was written with older adult communities in mind but applies more broadly to preaching for those who increasingly make up the majority of church members in this era of the continued "graying" of the church.

2 See chapter 8 for more ideas on creating sacred space.

3 For a helpful reflection on loss and meaning at the end of life, see Dawn DeVries, "The Spiritual Tasks of Aging towards Death," *Interpretation* 75 (July 2021): 227–35.

4 Walter J. Burghardt, "Aging: A Long Loving Look at the Real," in *Graying Gracefully: Preaching to Older Adults*, ed. William J. Carl Jr. (Louisville, KY: Westminster John Knox, 1997), 27.

5 Burghardt, 26, 27.

6 Cynthia M. Campbell, "Waiting on the Lord: Reflecting on Scripture near the End of Life," in Carl, *Graying Gracefully*, 74.

7 Campbell, 74.

8 Campbell, 79.

9 Barbara Brown Taylor, *The Preaching Life* (Lanham, MD: Rowman & Littlefield, 1993), 62.

10 David G. Buttrick, "Threescore, Ten, and Trouble: A Biblical View of Aging," in Carl, *Graying Gracefully*, 42.

11 Presbyterian Church, U.S.A., "A Brief Statement of Faith," in *Book of Confessions: Study Edition* (Louisville, KY: Westminster John Knox, 2017), 402.

12 William J. Carl Jr., "Questions That Need Answers: An Agenda for Preaching," in Carl, *Graying Gracefully*, 137.

Chapter 7: Holy Days and Holidays

1 J. Ellsworth Kalas, *Preaching the Calendar: Celebrating Holidays and Holy Days* (Louisville, KY: Westminster John Knox, 2004), 1.

2 Kalas, 7.

3 Laurence Hull Stookey, *Calendar: Christ's Time for the Church* (Nashville: Abingdon, 1996), 17.

4 Stookey, 19.

5 Kalas, *Preaching the Calendar*, 7–8.

6 There are many liturgies for Longest Night services (and services for healing and wholeness that can be adapted) available in liturgical resources found in books and on websites.

7 bell hooks, *All about Love: New Visions* (New York: William Morrow, 2001), 215.

8 From Charles Wesley, "Christ, Whose Glory Fills the Skies," in *Glory to God: Hymns, Psalms, and Spiritual Songs* (Louisville, KY: Westminster John Knox, 2013), hymn 662.

9 Rowan Williams, *Resurrection: Interpreting the Easter Gospel* (London: Darton, Longman & Todd, 1982), 96.

10 Kalas, *Preaching the Calendar*, 65.

11 Peter C. Bower, ed., *The Companion to the Book of Common Worship* (Louisville, KY: Geneva, 2003), 151.

12 Pope Pius XI, "*Quas primas*: On the Feast of Christ the King," Papal Encyclicals Online, December 11, 1925, https://www.papal encyclicals.net/pius11/p11prima.htm.

13 As quoted in John M. Buchanan, "Teaching Moments," *Christian Century* 122 (September 20, 2005): 3.

14 Julian of Norwich, "The Thirteenth Showing," in *Revelation of Love*, ed. and trans. John Skinner (New York: Image, 1996), 55.

15 James Calvin Davis, *American Liturgy: Finding Theological Meaning in the Holy Days of US Culture* (Eugene, OR: Cascade, 2021), 11.

16 Davis, 12–13.

17 See especially Martin Luther King Jr.'s classic sermon collection, *Strength to Love* (New York: Harper & Row, 1963).

18 Most communities now have book groups, service projects, and other ways of bringing people together across racial lines. One national organization, "Coming to the Table," has local chapters that meet "for truth-telling, building relationships, healing, and taking action to dismantle inequitable systems and structures based on race." See Coming to the Table, "About Us," accessed June 5, 2022, https://comingtothetable.org/about-us/.

19 Kalas, *Preaching the Calendar*, 76.

20 The Barna Group, "The State of Pastors 2021: Pastors Survey," Barna.com, October 2021, https://www.barna.com/research/pastors-quitting-ministry/.

21 See Leah D. Schade, *Preaching in the Purple Zone: Ministry in the Red-Blue Divide* (Lanham, MD: Rowman & Littlefield, 2019).

22 Stookey, *Calendar*, 33.

Chapter 9: Weddings and Divorces

1 Robert Burns, "A Red, Red Rose," Scottish Poetry Library, accessed January 17, 2022, https://www.scottishpoetrylibrary.org.uk/poem/red-red-rose/.

2 Louis de Bernières, *Captain Corelli's Mandolin* (New York: Vintage, 2001), 344–45.

3 Max Ehrmann, "Desiderata," in *The Desiderata of Happiness: A Collection of Philosophical Poems* (New York: Crown, 1948), 11.

4 Judith S. Wallerstein and Sandra Blakeslee, *The Good Marriage: How and Why Love Lasts* (New York: Warner, 1995), 334.

5 Gillian Flynn, "The Marriage Is the Real Mystery," *Morning Edition*, National Public Radio, June 5, 2012, https://www.npr.org/2012/06/05/154288241/the-marriage-is-the-real-mystery-in-gone-girl.

6 Andreas Capellanus, *The Art of Courtly Love*, ed. John Jay Parry (New York: Columbia University Press, 1941), 100. Quoted in Kimberly Long, *From This Day Forward: Rethinking the Christian Wedding* (Louisville, KY: Westminster John Knox, 2016), 41.

7 Ruth A. Meyers, "Christian Marriage and Funeral Services as Rites of Passage," *Oxford Research Encyclopedias*, published online May 9, 2016, https://oxfordre.com/view/10.1093/acrefore/9780199340378.001.0001/acrefore-9780199340378-e-15.

8 Meyers.

9 Mark Searle and Kenneth W. Stevenson, *Documents of the Marriage Liturgy* (Collegeville, MN: Liturgical, 1992), 216–17. Words of liturgy are quoted by Kimberly Long, with modernized spelling for easier reading, in *From This Day Forward*, 77.

10 *Book of Common Worship* (Louisville, KY: Westminster John Knox, 1993), 842.

11 *Book of Common Worship* (1993), 842.

12 *Book of Common Worship* (1993), 843.

13 *Book of Common Worship* (1993), 848.

14 Martin Luther, *The Estate of Marriage* (1522), as excerpted in Susan C. Karant-Nunn and Merry E. Wiesner-Hanks, eds. and trans., *Luther on Women: A Sourcebook* (Cambridge, UK: Cambridge University, 2003), 100.

15 Long, *From This Day Forward*, 88.

16 Long, 131.

17 Gene Robinson, *God Believes in Love: Straight Talk about Gay Marriage* (New York: Vintage, 2013), 11.

Chapter 10: Crises and Tragedies

1 Anne Quigley, "There Is a Longing in Our Hearts," in *Glory to God: Hymns, Psalms, and Spiritual Songs* (Louisville, KY: Westminster John Knox, 2013), hymn 470.

2 For the theory and practice of the exegesis of your congregation, see Lenora Tubbs Tisdale, *Preaching as Local Theology and Folk Art* (Minneapolis: Fortress, 1997). For a simplified process, along with other helpful exercises for preaching, see Thomas H. Troeger and Leonora Tubbs Tisdale, *A Sermon Workbook: Exercises in the Art and Craft of Preaching* (Nashville: Abingdon, 2013).

3 Joni S. Sancken, *Words That Heal: Preaching Hope to Wounded Souls* (Nashville: Abingdon, 2019), 1–2.

4 Sancken, 13.

5 Thomas G. Long, *What Shall We Say? Evil, Suffering, and the Crisis of Faith* (Grand Rapids, MI: Eerdmans, 2011), 126.

6 Long, 128.

7 Sancken, *Words That Heal*, 76.

8 Long, *What Shall We Say?*, 133.

9 Long, 139.

10 Long, 142.

11 Long, 145.

12 Elie Wiesel, "The Holocaust as a Literary Inspiration," in *Dimensions of the Holocaust* (Evanston, IL: Northwestern University Press, 1977), 9. Quoted in Shelly Rambo, *Spirit and Trauma: A Theology of Remaining* (Louisville, KY: Westminster John Knox, 2010), 23.

13 Rambo, *Spirit and Trauma*, 40.

14 Rambo, 40.

Working Preacher BOOKS

Good Preaching
Changes Lives

Working Preacher Books is a partnership between Luther Seminary, WorkingPreacher.org, and Fortress Press.

Books in the Series

Preaching from the Old Testament by Walter Brueggemann

Leading with the Sermon: Preaching as Leadership by William H. Willimon

The Gospel People Don't Want to Hear: Preaching Challenging Messages by Lisa Cressman

A Lay Preacher's Guide: How to Craft a Faithful Sermon by Karoline M. Lewis

Preaching Jeremiah: Announcing God's Restorative Passion by Walter Brueggemann

Preaching the Headlines: Pitfalls and Possibilities by Lisa L. Thompson

Honest to God Preaching: Talking Sin, Suffering, and Violence by Brent A. Strawn

Writing for the Ear, Preaching from the Heart by Donna Giver-Johnston

The Peoples' Sermon: Preaching as a Ministry of the Whole Congregation by Shauna K. Hannan

Real People, Real Faith: Preaching Biblical Characters by Cindy Halvorson

The Visual Preacher: Proclaiming an Embodied Word by Steve Thomason

Divine Laughter: Preaching and the Serious Business of Humor by Karl N. Jacobson and Rolf A. Jacobson

For Every Matter under Heaven: Preaching on Special Occasions by Beverly Zink-Sawyer and Donna Giver-Johnston